CONTENTS

CONTENTS

BAR AND BEVERAGE MANAGEMENT

DR. Raj Kumar Singh
D.H.C.T. Mgmt. (W.B.)
P.G.D.B. Mgmt. (U.P.)
C.F.N. (Delhi)
MHCIMA (London)
Ph.D. (Management)
Director
'SAMS' Institute of Hotel Management,
Varanasi

AMAN PUBLICATIONS
NEW DELHI (INDIA)

Published by
Rajiv Jain for Aman Publications
LG-4A, Ganpati Bhawan,
4675-B/21, Ansari Road,
Darya Ganj, Delhi - 110002
PH: 23255012, 23282127
E-mail: sshjbs@yahoo.com

(Reprint) : 2010
ISBN-81-8204-015-9 (PB)

SOLE DISTRIBUTOR
JINDAL BOOK SERVICES
LG-4A, Ganpati Bhawan,
4675-B/21, Ansari Road,
Darya Ganj, Delhi - 110002

Laser Typesetting by:
S.M. Graphics, Delhi,

Printed by:
NCT Printers & Publishers , Delhi, India

Bar and Beverage Management

Preface

Alcohols and beverages play an important role in restaurant or food service operation by being a key profit centre. Profitable bar and beverage service is crucial to the success of many operations. The ability to mix a drink does not guarantee success — the management of the bar does. By explaining how to operate the beverage part of a restaurant as well as how to serve alcohol students will learn the tools necessary to create a successful beverage operation. In today's market, whether running a stand-alone business or one incorporated into a restaurant, hotel, or food service operation, the successful bar operator needs to have product and equipment knowledge, management savvy, marketing skills, insight into the latest trends, and, of course, a strong grasp of mixology.

This book is an essential guide to successful bar and beverage management. It has the most up-to-date material on managing a beverage operation, bar equipment, sanitation and bar setup, managing inventory, and planning for profit. Informative and practical in approach, it helps readers understand and appreciate the intricacies of how to manage a bar and beverage operation profitably.

1

Introduction

Throughout history, alcoholic beverages have played an important role in most cultures. People drank them for many good reasons-for food and health, worship and celebration, pleasure and fellowship, wisdom and truth. As civilisation developed, the inns, alehouses, and taverns were central to the growth of towns, travel, and the communication of ideas.

Earliest Wines

Perhaps 8,000 to 10,000 years ago, someone discovered that fermented fruit or grain or milk or rice tasted good, made one happy, or both. The Bible mentions wine consumption in both Old and New Testaments. When Noah settled down after the flood, he planted a vineyard ". . . and he drank of the wine and was drunken." With all its benefits and hazards, alcohol was a universal feature of early civilisations.

At least one legend claims that wine was discovered accidentally, by a neglected member of a Persian king's harem. She attempted to end her loneliness by ending her life, drinking from a jar marked "Poison." It contained grapes that had fermented. She felt so much better after drinking the liquid that she gave a cup of it to the king, who named it "the delightful poison" and welcomed her back into active harem life.

Early peoples all over the world fermented anything that would ferment-honey, grapes, grains, dates, rice, sugarcane, milk, palms, peppers, berries, sesame seeds, pomegranates. We know that grapes were cultivated as early as 6000 B.C., both in the Middle East and Asia. The Egyptians, Phoenicians, and Chinese were tending their vines at about the same time. It is believed that the ancient Greeks got their viticulture knowledge from the Egyptians, beginning to make wine about 2000 B.C.

The practice of aging wines was first discovered by the Greeks, in cylinders known as amphora. Made of clay, they were remarkably airtight. Fifteen hundred years later, the Romans tried a similar method, but their clay was more porous and didn't work as well. So they began coating their clay vessels with tar on the insides, a process known as pitching. Yes, it prevented air from mixing with wine, but can you imagine what the addition of tar must have done to the quality of the wine?

By 1000 B.C., grapevines were found in Sicily and Northern Africa. Within the next 500 years, they reached the Iberian Peninsula, Southern France, and even Southern Russia. Conquering Saracen (Arab) tribes in the Middle Ages brought both winemaking and distillation skills with them. In fact, the words "alcohol" and "still" are Arabic in origin.

As the Roman Empire spread, it brought grapes to Northern Europe, too. After the fall of the Roman Empire, the Catholic Church was the most prominent promoter of viticulture. Monasteries became the vanguards of wine production and knowledge, because wine was needed both in everyday life and in sacramental activities. The

Portuguese are credited with shipping the first corked bottles of wine to England, but not until the year 1780. In many cultures, people associated intoxicating beverages with wisdom. Early Persians discussed all matters of importance twice-once when they were sober and once when they were drunk.

Saxons in ancient England opened their council meetings by passing around a large, stone mug of beer. Greeks held their famous symposiums-philosophical discussions-during hours of after-dinner drinking. In fact, the word "symposium" means "drinking together." As the Roman historian Pliny summed it up, "In vino veritas" ("in wine there is truth").

Alcoholic beverages, often in combination with herbs, have been used for centuries as medicines and tonics. Indeed, herbs and alcohol were among the few ways of treating or preventing disease until about a century ago. But probably the most important historic use of alcoholic beverages was also the simplest: as food and drink. Bread and ale, or bread and wine, were the staples of any meal for an ordinary person, with the drink considered food.

For centuries, these hearty beverages provided up to half the calories needed for a day's heavy labor. And they were considered the only liquids fit to drink, with good reason. Household water was commonly polluted. Milk could cause "milk sickness" (tuberculosis). But beer, ale, and wine were disease-free, tasty, and thirst-quenching, crucial qualities in societies that preserved food with salt, and washed it down a diet of starches.

Both wines and grapevines were imported from France to the New World in the 1700s. As U.S. Minister to France, Thomas Jefferson was one of the primary supporters of the fledgling winemaking industry, and tried (passionately but unsuccessfully) to grow his own grapes at Monticello. By the early 1900s, there were about 1,700 wineries dotting the United States, mostly small, family-owned businesses.

Wine was still considered an effete beverage until the 1800s, when Italian immigrants came to the United States with their home winemaking skills and a hospitable culture that accepted wine as a simple, everyday part of mealtimes and celebrations. Many of today's best-known California winemakers, with names like Gallo and Mondavi, are descendants of these immigrant families.

Role of Religion

Early beers, ales, and wines were considered gifts from the gods, that is, miracle products with magical powers. People used them universally in religious rites, and they still do. The Israelites of the Old Testament offered libations to Jehovah. Greeks and Romans honored Bacchus, god of wine. Christians used wine in the sacrament of communion. Primitive peoples used fermented beverages in their sacred rites.

Victories, weddings, and other sacred and joyous occasions were celebrated with "mellow wine" or endless supplies of ale (the word "bridal" comes from bride + ale). Camaraderie and fellowship were acknowledged with a "loving cup," passed around the table and shared by all until it was emptied.

Of all alcoholic beverages, wine has the greatest religious connection. In the book Religion and Wine: A Cultural History of Wine-Drinking in the United States, the author, Robert Fuller, traces the development of winemaking from the French Huguenots, Protestants who settled along the East Coast of North America in the 1500s, to the Pilgrims in Plymouth Bay in the 1600s to the Franciscan friars and Jesuit priests who built the early missions in California during the 1700s and 1800s.

Whether these early Americans were Baptists, Methodists, or Mormons, they permitted and enjoyed limited wine consumption as part of their worship. According to Fuller, the United States did not have "grape-juice Protestants" (who decried the alcohol content of wine and replaced it in ceremonies with grape juice) until the late eighteenth century. Interestingly, this alternative was first developed by Thomas Welch, a dentist and Methodist minister. His name later became a famous trademark for juice products.

At that time, attitudes about alcohol changed as some religious groups (Fuller calls them "ascetic Christians") began to espouse the theory that the road to heaven required total self-discipline, including the denial of all earthly pleasures. It was feared by some that consuming alcohol would weaken sensibility, ethics, and moral values, and diminish selfcontrol in an age where many churches sought greater control over their members.

On the other hand, some religious groups felt equally strongly that rituals using wine could mediate God's presence and foster greater enjoyment of what life had to offer. These included Roman Catholics, Eastern Orthodox, Episcopalians, and Lutherans. And so the rift widened.

Since the 1800s, the relationship between alcohol and religion has been the subject of debate and ambivalence. As recently as 1990, California winemaker Robert Mondavi designed a new label for his wines, to include a paragraph extolling the beverage's longtime role in culture and religion. In part, it read, "Wine has been with us since the beginning of civilisation. It is a temperate, civilised, sacred, romantic mealtime beverage recommended in the Bible . . ." Mondavi was prohibited from using this wording by the U.S. Bureau of Alcohol, Tobacco and Firearms.

History of Beer

As far back as 6000 B.C., Babylonian scribes included beer recipes in their writings, and the ancient Egyptians made note of Ramses III, the pharaoh whose annual sacrifice of about 30,000 gallons of beer appeased "thirsty gods." Before 1850, the beverage preference in the United States was ale, which had been popular in England. It was made like beer, but fermented more quickly, at higher temperatures than beer.

The word "beer" comes from the ancient Latin word "biber," a slang term for the beverage made by fermenting grain, with hops for flavoring. Back then, biber was considered lower-class compared to ale, which was made in similar fashion but without the addition of hops.

Just about every civilisation has made some type of beer, from whatever grain or root or plant was available in abundance. African tribes made their beer from millet; in Japan, it was rice; in Europe, North and South America, the chief ingredient was barley. The brew was hearty, filling, and provided calories and nutrients to fuel manual labor. The significance of beer in the average person's diet was demonstrated at the landing of the Mayflower at Plymouth, in what is now Massachusetts. The Pilgrims were headed for Virginia, but the ship was running out of beer. So they were "hasted ashore and made to drink water that the seamen might have more beer," wrote Governor Bradford later.

Beer production and sales played colorful parts of U.S. history. The first American brewery was opened in Lower Manhattan by the Dutch West Indies Company in 1632. There is speculation that the crude streets of New Amsterdam were first paved to help the horse-drawn beer wagons make better progress, since they were so often stuck in the mud! Brewing became an aristocratic and popular business. William Penn, the Quaker leader who founded the state of Pennsylvania, Revolutionary War leaders Samuel Adams and Ethan Allen, and even George Washington, all were brewery owners.

By the mid-nineteenth century, brewing dynasties, that are still household names among today's beer-drinkers had begun in the United States. In Detroit, Michigan, Bernard Stroh, from a beer-making family in Rhineland, Germany, opened his brewing company in 1850. Five years later, Frederick Miller purchased an existing facility, Best's Brewery in Milwaukee, Wisconsin. In St. Louis, Eberhard Anheuser purchased a struggling brewery in 1860. His daughter married Adolphus Busch, a German immigrant whose family supplied grains and hops, and the mighty Anheuser-Busch Company was born. A dozen years later, another German immigrant from the Rhineland, Adolph Coors, started to brew beer in Colorado.

The Germans brought with them a different brewing style that produced a lighter beer known as lager, which is more pale and clear in appearance than ale and has a drier flavor. Its name comes from a German word for "storage" or "storehouse," since it was routinely stored for several months in cold temperatures before serving. Making lager-style beer required ice, so it was typically brewed in winter and stored until summer, when the demand was highest. Milwaukee emerged as the nation's brewing center for the most practical reason: ice was easily available from Lake Michigan, and there were plenty of local caves to store the beer.

When refrigerators and icemakers were invented, lager could be brewed anytime, anyplace. Heat was just as important as cold to the fast-growing beer-making industry. The French chemist Louis Pasteur discovered in the 1800s that, like milk or cider, beer could be heated to sufficient temperature to kill harmful bacteria without diminishing the quality of the brew. This process of pasteurisation allowed beer to be bottled for shipment.

History of Distilled Spirits

The art of distillation-first heating, then cooling and condensing liquids to extract and concentrate their alcohol content-was known in crude form even in ancient times. The Chinese and peoples of the East Indies distilled liquids and used the resulting potions for medicinal purposes as early as 800 B.C. About the time the Pilgrims ran out of beer at Plymouth Rock, these forms of concentrated alcohol were coming into favor in Europe.

Distilled spirits made from fermented liquids were many times more potent than the original liquids. The first ones were called aqua vitae (water of life) and were used as medicines, but they were quickly assimilated into society as beverages. Highland Scots and Irish distillers made whiskey. The French distilled wine to make brandy. A Dutch doctor's experiments produced gin, alcohol flavored with the juniper berry. In Russia and Poland, the distilled spirit was vodka. In the West Indies, rum was made from sugarcane, while in Mexico, Spaniards distilled the Indians' native drink to make mescal, the great-granddaddy of today's tequila.

With increasing supplies of spirits and their high alcohol content, excessive drinking became a national problem in several European countries. In England, cheap gin became the drink of the poor. They could-and did-get "drunk for a penny, dead drunk for twopence," as one gin mill advertised. This particular mill, in the same advertisement, mentioned that it also provided "free straw" (a bed of hay) for sleeping it off. Across the Atlantic, Americans welcomed the new spirits, and it wasn't long before rum became the most popular drink and New England became a leading manufacturer.

However, in 1791, the new U.S. Congress enacted the first tax on whiskey production. Many of the distillers, still trying to recover financially from the Revolutionary War, did not have much money and refused to pay the taxes. By 1794, President Washington had a real problem on his hands. He mustered 12,000 troops and marched into Pennsylvania to avert the so-called Whiskey Rebellion. It ended without a shot being fired, but many angry distillers packed up and moved further west to enjoy greater freedom and avoid future confrontations. In fact, relocation to the limestone soils of Tennessee and Kentucky led some of these early distillers to a real gold mine: the cold, clear water supplies of these areas, which are still famous for their whiskey production.

The spirit soon became known as "bourbon," since some of the first distillers set up shop in Bourbon County, Kentucky. As the American West was settled, whiskey-easier to store and transport than beer or wine, and much in demand-became a very popular commodity in the trade-andbarter commerce of frontier life.

Distillation gained momentum as the process was refined. Rectification, or distilling a liquid more than once, yielded a much cleaner and almost 100 percent pure spirits than previous efforts. Before rectification was perfected, spirits contained flavor impurities. Herbs, honey and/or flowers were added to mask them. After rectification, these items were also routinely added, but now, to enhance the flavor. Some of today's grand liqueurs are the results of these early flavor concoctions. Cognac, for instance, was a pale, acidic French wine for which there was little public demand . . . until it was concentrated in the 1600s as an eau de vie, French for aqua vitae. It became enormously popular, and still is today.

Present Condition of Beverage Industry

Since 1990, there has been a gradual decline in alcohol consumption in all its forms-beer, wine, and spirits. Expert observers relate the drop to a change in lifestyle for many busy Americans, many of whom turned their focus on health, fitness, and job success. These people have stopped smoking, they exercise, they watch their weight and their cholesterol count, and they keep their heads clear during working hours. The "three-Martini lunch" is now a rarity, replaced by bottled waters or fruit juice or sometimes a single glass of wine. These people are moderate drinkers, limiting their consumption to the one or two drinks a day. At the same time, they are very much interested in the quality of whatever drink they choose. When they do imbibe, they tend to choose premium or superpremium liquors and wines. "Drinking less but drinking better" has become the norm.

The health-and-fitness enthusiast is looking for lighter drinks, those perceived to have less alcohol and fewer calories. Sales of spirits (high in alcohol and calories) continue to decline. "White goods" (vodka, gin, tequila, and rum) generally do better than "brown goods" (bourbon, scotch, and other whiskies) even though they all have similar alcohol contents. But according to Beverage Digest magazine, which tracks U.S. beverage consumption figures, Americans drank the highest amount of distilled spirits-two gallons per person, per year-back in the 1970s. Today's consumption figures are more like 1.2 or 1.3 gallons per person, per year, and have been since 1993.

Wine enjoyed its largest upsurge in popularity in the 1980s, reaching a high of 2.4 gallons per person, per year. Wine is still popular and boasts a loyal following of hobbyists and collectors, but overall consumption has leveled off at about 2 gallons per person, per year. Despite jam-packed supermarket wine section shelves and all kinds of exotic choices, the three best sellers continue to be Chardonnay, Cabernet Sauvignon, and White Zinfandel. Beer sales look mighty impressive when compared to wine and spirits!

For the last decade Americans have consumed more than 22 gallons of beer per person, per year. Trends during this time include the so-called light beers, which are lower in alcohol and calories than their "regular" counterparts; dry beers (crisply flavored, and touting "no aftertaste"); and nonalcoholic beers, with about two dozen brands on the market in the early 1990s. Light beers now account for about 40 percent of all beer sales in the United States.

Imported beers and beers from small, regional breweries (microbreweries) have gained substantial followings, and there's a small but lively home-brewing hobbyist market. In most major cities, you'll find at least one beer-making store where home brewers can buy equipment and supplies and get advice. For a fee, some allow you to brew on-site, let the beer age in their storage tanks, then come back and bottle your own creation yourself! Smart restaurateurs now offer wines by the glass in addition to wines by the bottle, realising that today's diners may not want to order a full bottle.

Customers may also ask for a nonalcoholic drink. Offerings include mineral waters, nonalcoholic beers, soft drinks, juice drinks, and even no-alcohol mixed drinks. Some bars have invented "mocktails," alcohol-free versions of the Bloody Mary, Piña Colada, and others, mixed and served with the same care and flair as their house specialties. This does not mean that Martinis or Gin and Tonics are obsolete, or that fewer people are patronising bars or ordering drinks with their meals. There has been renewed interest in the traditional cocktails (Martini, Bloody Mary, Screwdriver) and "tall drinks" (Scotch and Soda or Bourbon and Soda, Gina and Tonic or Vodka and Tonic).

There is also strong interest in call brands, the slang term for premium brands that are asked for-or, "called for"-by name. Superpremium imports, like single-malt scotches, Irish whiskeys, Cognac and Armagnac brandies, also have loyal followings. They are popular with customers who have developed a taste for and interest in "buying the best," and are willing to pay more for it. They are also interested in experimenting -trying new brands and learning more about beverages. By contrast, most brown goods customers are in the upper-age groups and are comfortable with their reliable favorites, such as Scotch and Soda or Bourbon and Water.

New drinks will be invented, new twists added to old favorites. Managing a bar means keeping your finger on the pulse of the market and making the changes necessary to stay ahead. Let's look next at a few different types of beverage service. Though it is impossible to divide bars into just a few categories-there are almost as many variations as there are bars-certain kinds have distinct characteristics and styles of service, and it may be revealing to see how they differ and what they have in common.

The simplest kind of beverage enterprise is the bar that serves beverages alone, with no food service except snacks: peanuts, pretzels, cheese and crackers. This type of bar serves beer or wine or mixed drinks or any combination of the three, plus nonalcoholic beverages. It may be a neighborhood gathering place, a way station for commuters on their homeward treks, a bar at an airport or bus terminal or bowling alley.

Business at such bars typically has a predictable flow: a daily pattern of peaks and valleys, a weekly pattern of slow days and heavy days, with the heavy days related to paydays and days off. There may also be seasonal patterns. In airports and bus terminals, business is geared to daily, weekly, and seasonal travel patterns, and according to the time of day; light beverages are served mornings and afternoons, heartier drinks are ordered as the working day ends. Because only one type of product is sold, and because business is generally predictable, the operation of a beverage-only bar is relatively simple, from production to staffing and purchasing to keeping track of the beverages, money, and profits.

This type of bar also usually has a specific reason for success, perhaps its location, its reputation as a friendly place (or for pouring well-made drinks), or simply a lack of competition; maybe it has just "always been the place where everybody goes." Often such bars thrive by being the same as they always were. Customers become sentimental about them and would not tolerate change.

That said, as the mood of the country changes, many neighborhood bars are adding food to their offerings. Hotel chains such as Marriott, Radisson, and Hyatt have phased out their cocktail-only lounges in favor of food and beverage combinations. The decision is practical: some states do not allow beverage sales without food sales; other bar owners have decided it's simply more responsible to offer people food if they will be drinking. Master concessionaires, such as Host Marriott, now run more than 1,800 restaurants in 73 airports, and the trend has been to upgrade these facilities to pour more premium beverages, serve better food, partner with brewpubs, and offer entertainment for travelers awaiting their flights.

In short, beverage-only bars are definitely a minority today. Although some are highly profitable, most bars find that serving liquor alone is not enough to attract and keep customers. So the majority of bars offer something else-entertainment or food or both.

Entertainment Combinations

Bars offering entertainment range from the neighborhood bar with pool, pinball, dartboards, or giant TV screens to nightclubs with big-name entertainers and comedy clubs and ballrooms with big bands. In between are cocktail lounges and nightclubs with live entertainment-piano bars, country-andwestern dancing, jazz or folk duos, or rousing rock-and-roll groups. This concept must include the decision to make room for a stage area, sound system, and dance floor. And having entertainment means hiring someone knowledgeable to book the bands or entertainers that people will want to see (negotiating contracts at a fair but affordable price) and always thinking ahead to the next fad or hottest music trend to attract the fickle public.

A concept that includes regular entertainment of any kind also includes the fixed costs and additional financial risk of hiring and paying the entertainers. In most cases, the entertainment may draw the crowd, but it is the drinks that provide the profits. If there is a cover charge, an admission fee per person paid at the door, at least part of it is likely to go to the entertainers. The fortunes of this type of bar will rise and fall with the popularity of its entertainers, unless the place has something else going for it.

Probably the most stable type of bar/entertainment combo is the smaller place with an attractive ambience, good drinks, and local entertainment to draw a loyal, local crowd. Its success potential is much the same as the baronly enterprise. Larger operations featuring out-of-town entertainers have a higher but riskier profit potential. It is likely to be either feast or famine. The bar gears up for each crowd with temporary extra help, a large investment in liquor inventory, and possibly extra security personnel. Weather, holidays, location, and weeknight versus weekend crowds all heavily impact this type of business.

Casinos are another enduring combination of entertainment and beverage service. Today's casinos may be run by a huge corporation or a Native American tribal council, and may include everything from big-name stage productions and professional boxing matches to restaurants and nongambling arcades that attract families instead of adults only.

Sports bars offer a different type of entertainment. They center on the viewing of popular sporting events, such as Monday Night Football, or special events like hockey finals or the World Series. Equipped with large television screens (or plenty of smaller ones strategically placed), the sports bar often sets a fixed price or cover charge to guarantee a good profit because customer turnover is so small. Large sports bars often serve a menu of full-course meals, and many take reservations in advance of popular events like a professional boxing match or a Triple Crown horse race.

The cigar bar is another trendy addition to the beverage scene-and a profitable one, too. Men and an increasing number of women are enjoying high-priced cigars, and restaurateurs have seized the opportunity to recommend premium spirits, wines, beers, and after-dinner drinks to accompany them. The cigar boom is not legal in all venues, since smoking is prohibited in many public places by local ordinance. But the places that install heavyduty fans and humidors and offer extensive cigar selections-plus single-malt Scotches, small-batch Bourbons, Cognacs and Ports-are filling an interesting, upscale niche. Sometimes, they are private clubs that charge membership fees.

Combinations of Food and Beverage

The most common form of beverage operation is one that is linked with some kind of food service. One type is the restaurant/bar, where drinks and wine are part of the meal service, served by the same wait staff that serves the meal. The bar is often used as the waiting area for the restaurant during busy times. Drinks may be poured at a service bar out of public view or at a pickup station in a bar that serves customers while they are waiting for a table. The major portion of the sales comes from the food service. However, the beverage sales often turn the profit for the enterprise. The only added costs are for the wine and liquor, and the bartender and a minimum investment in equipment; the other necessities-service personnel and the facility itself-are built in to the restaurant operation.

Another type of food-beverage combination is the bar that offers light food in addition to drinks. In this case, the beverages and the bar atmosphere dominate, and the major sales volume comes from the bar. But the food is a nice sidelight that attracts customers and prolongs their stay. Typical menu items are appetizers: nachos, chips or crudités and dips, spiced chicken wings, stuffed potato skins.

A special variation of the food-beverage combination is the wine bar, which first appeared during the 1970s as Americans discovered and learned to appreciate wines. Here the customer can choose from a selection of wines by the glass or by the bottle, beginning with inexpensive house wines and going up in quality and price as far as the entrepreneur cares to go. Some wine bars offer inexpensive one-ounce "tastes" to allow guests to sample a number of wines. A full menu can be served, or fruit and cheese platters and upscale hors d'oeuvres.

There are inherent problems in running wine bars. The first is, of course, that serving only wine tends to limit the clientele to wine lovers. In some urban areas, there are enough wine enthusiasts to support a profitable enterprise; they respond to quality and expertise, and they attend and appreciate special tastings and classes and wine-centered celebrations. This enthusiasm, however, raises a second difficulty: purchasing appropriate wines requires an expertise few people have, and may require a financial investment few are willing to make.

As a result, many wine bars serve liquor and beer as well. This broadens their appeal and allows them to realise the necessary profit margin. In effect, they are simply bars that specialise in wine sales and wine knowledge. Other wine bars may broaden their offerings by serving meals, in effect becoming restaurants with an emphasis on wines. Some also sell wines at retail, offering customers discounts for volume (one case or more) purchases. This combination of on-premise service and take-home sales is not an option everywhere. Beverage laws in many areas do not allow it.

Beer aficionados also have their own version of the wine bar. At a brewpub, beer is brewed and served right on the premises-fresh, natural beers and ales, strong in flavor and aroma, with special seasonal offerings. Developed by small individual entrepreneurs and hobbyists, the beverage sets the theme of the restaurant. At least one shiny brew kettle is likely to be a major part of the décor, and the menu typically contains hearty, casual cuisine chosen to complement the beer. As popular as they are in many areas of the United States, brewpubs are not legal everywhere, as some states still do not allow manufacture and sale of alcoholic beverages on the same premises.

A popular type of food-beverage combination links a bar and a restaurant on an equal, semi-independent basis, with a common roof, theme, management team, and services that complement each other. The bar and restaurant areas are housed in separate portions of the building, and they may be open at slightly different hours to serve both the drop-in bar customer and the mealtime patron. The food/drink sales ratio is likely to reflect an equal status of food and drink, with bar and restaurant each doing better than it would without the other. In many cases, neither side could make a go of it alone, but together the customer attraction and income are doubled, while the overhead costs are split between them.

Hotel Beverage Operations

In hotels, the beverage operation differs in many ways from the bar or the bar-restaurant combination. There may be three or four bars under one roof, each with a different purpose and a different ambience-say a lobby bar, a cocktail lounge, a restaurant bar, a nightclub with dancing. In addition, there is room service, with a food menu that includes mixed drinks, beer, wine, and Champagne. Above all, there is banquet service, catering to conference, convention, and reception needs. Typically, the client makes beverage choices in advance of the event, which are served from portable bars by extra personnel hired for the occasion.

And in individual rooms, don't forget the minibar. Many hotels have installed them for the convenience of guests, an in-room refreshment center without the room service waiter. The minibar is really nothing more than a small refrigerator with an icemaker-although many have classy mock mahogany exterior cabinets-stocked with a small inventory of snacks and drinks.

There are three keys to profitable minibar use, according to Lodging magazine. The unit must be installed so that it is easy to use and its contents are clearly visible, and a reliable system must be in place for prompt restocking of cabinets and correct billing of guests. Perhaps most important, customers must be enticed to somehow overlook the high prices of minibar goods! Its in-room convenience means the hotel can charge double, or even triple, what the same goods would cost elsewhere on the same property.

Food and Beverage Directors of large hotels say the minibar has become a necessary amenity, even though it could be argued that it does siphon some business away from the hotel's other food and beverage venues, especially room service. But overall, the minibar is not a major moneymaker for most hotels; and, interestingly, the most common minibar purchase is not alcohol of any kind, but bottled water.

Perhaps the most daunting challenge of hotel beverage service is its diversity, coupled with the up-and-down nature of demand. Since a hotel's primary clientele is its overnight guests, demand for beverages rises and falls according to the occupancy rate. This, too, is unpredictable: a hotel can be completely full for a convention and yet have very little bar trade, depending on the kind of convention it is hosting. On the other hand, a very low occupancy rate may net a lot of bar business. Again, it just depends on who the hotel guests are.

Resort and luxury hotels often have several bars and restaurants, with a variety of entertainment, food, and drink, to keep the hotel guests spending money on the premises, as well as to attract an outside clientele. On the other hand, a small commercial hotel in a big city may need only one bar with several stations to serve its lobby customers, its cocktail lounge, coffee shop, dining room, and room service.

Airline Beverage Service

Another type of beverage service that must adapt to special conditions is that on airline flights. The restrictions of space, time, weight, and equipment are formidable. (Cruise lines and passenger trains have similar storage limitations.) Of necessity, their drink menus are limited. Liquors, beers, wines, and a few types of cocktail mixes are handed out in small individual bottles or cans. The cups are nesting, plastic disposables, except in first and business class cabins. Flight attendants push a beverage cart down the aisle and, working from both ends, can garnish glasses and fill them with ice, pour beverages or hand out the individual-sized drink components, and collect the money. The process is a marvel of organisation. Tight control systems follow the little bottles everywhere, since they are extraordinarily tempting to both airline employees and customers. For higher-paying passengers, drinks are free and service typically includes real glassware, a choice or wines, Champagne for breakfast, and sometimes specialty drinks.

Grouping types of beverage service into these rather arbitrary categories does not really adequately describe the character of individual enterprises. Many establishments do not fit handily into a specific category, and those within categories can be as different as day and night. Yet all categories have certain similarities. They all sell alcoholic beverages. They have similar staff structures, patterns of purchasing and inventory, and ways of controlling the merchandise. They all must meet certain government requirements and operate within certain government regulations. Even the prices charged for the same drinks are not wildly different from one type of place to another. Still, no two bar and beverage operations are alike, unless they are part of a chain. The successful business is one that meets the needs and desires of a certain clientele and strives to be deliberately different from others serving a similar clientele in order to stand out in the competition for customers. Other major reasons for the wide variety of bar operations are simple: the special circumstances of each operation and the personalities, desires, and budgets of their owners. But to be successful, the entrepreneur must put clientele above all else in shaping his or her enterprise.

Characteristics of Alcoholic Beverages

Alcoholic beverages all share the common feature of being produced through anaerobic fermentation of plant-derived carbohydrate materials by yeasts. Sugars are converted to alcohol (ethanol) and carbon dioxide by these fungi, which also impart characteristic flavours and aromas to the beverage. Depending upon what fermentable material is used, and the method by which the materials are processed, alcoholic beverages may be classified as being wines, beers, or spirits. Many countries in which they are produced regulate the production of most spirits, beer, and wine and carefully control taxation of these alcoholic beverages.

Wine

Wines are alcoholic beverages that have been fermented from fleshy fruits (e.g., apples, grapes, peaches, and plums), although most often from the cultivated grape *Vitis vinifera* (family Vitaceae) and related species. While the vast majority of wines are made from grapes, wines may also be made from the vegetative parts of certain plants.

Wines are made by harvesting ripened grapes from farms known as vineyards. The timing of the harvest is critical, since a balance of accumulated sugar, acids, and other grape flavour components reaches an optimal level to ultimately produce a fine wine. If the grapes are harvested too soon or too late, there is the possibility of producing a lower quality wine.

Characteristics of Alcoholic Beverages

Beverage	Fermented Materials	Carbonated?	Distilled?	Other Features
Beers				
Ales	Barley malt, wheat, rice	Yes	No	Warm fermented
Stout	Highly kilned (dark) malt	Yes	No	An ale using dark malts
Lagers	Barley malt	Yes	No	Cold

				fermented
Weizen beers	Wheat malt	Yes	No	Wheat beers of Germany
Wines				
Red	Grapes fermented with skins	No	No	Served at room temperature
White	Grapes ented skins	No	No	ferm- without Served chilled
Port	Grapes	No	No/Yes	Fortified with alcohol/ cognac
Champagne	Grapes fermented without skins	Yes	No	A sparkling wine
Sparkling wines	Grapes	Yes	No	May be blended
Spirits				
Whiskeys				
Scotch (single malt)	Barley malt, often peat-smoked	No	Yes	Aged in oak casks
Rye	Rye (at least 51 percent)	No	Yes	Maximum 80 proof
Bourbon	Corn (at least 51 percent)	No	Yes	Sour mashed with bacteria
Gin	Malt, other grains with juniper cones	No	Yes	Flavoured
Rum	Sugarcane or molasses	No	Yes	Light or

				dark rums available
Tequila/ Mescal	Agave tequiliana stems	No	Yes	Traditional drinks of Mexico
Vodka	Malt, grains, potatoes	No	Yes	Few additional flavors
Brandy/ Cognac	Wines	No	Yes	Distilled wines
Liqueurs	Wines	No	Yes	Sweetened with added sugars
Other				
Sake	Rice	No	No	Double fermentation
Cider	Apples	Yes/No	No	May be flavored/ spiced
Mead	Honey	Yes/No	No	May be flavored/ spiced

Bunches of grapes are removed from the vines, usually by manual labour, and are brought to the winery for production. The grapes are passed through a mechanical destemmer that removes the nonfruit portions of the bunches, and the fruits are then crushed to express the juice from the fleshy berries. The liquid obtained from the crushed grapes is termed "must." The must is placed in either open or closed fermentation vessels (typically closed vessels in modern wineries) and readied for fermentation. If red wines are being made, the skins from the pressed grapes are also added to the fermentation vessel (the grape skins contribute reddish pigments to the finished wine); for white wine production, the skins are not used and only clear must is fermented.

The must that is ready to be fermented is then inoculated with a particular strain of yeast (*Saccharomyces cerevisiae*) that has been selected for wine fermentation. There are hundreds of different strains of wine yeast, each imparting a particular flavour during the fermentation. When complete, the fermentation will produce an alcohol content of approximately 12 to 14 percent alcohol by volume. Following fermentation, any suspended particulate material (the lees) is allowed to settle, and the clear wine is siphoned (or racked) to a new storage vessel, which is usually a large barrel made from white oak wood.

The wine is then conditioned in these barrels for a year or more, occasionally being racked to new oak barrels as the wine matures. Under these conditions, chemical reactions take place in the wine that add complexity to the flavor profile. Even contact with tannins in the walls of the barrel provides subtle and desirable flavor characteristics that lower quality wines conditioned in stainless steel vessels lack. Most wines are "still" (not carbonated), but sparkling wines are allowed to undergo another fermentation after they mature, and are bottled while this fermentation is occuring, thereby carbonating the wine. Champagne is one famous version of a sparkling (white) wine originally from the region of France known by that name.

Wines are bottled in glass containers and are usually sealed by inserting a compressed cork into the neck of the bottles. Wine is stored and further matured while laying on the side, so that the cork remains moist to maintain its airtight seal. Some wines should be consumed within a year or two of production; others need many years or decades to achieve their optimum flavor.

The wine industry is an extensive one, with major centers of production in France, California, Italy, Spain, and Germany, with additional developing centers of production in South Africa, Australia, Argentina, and

Chile. Although wine is vinted around the world, certain places are favored for wine production due to optimal climates and suitable land for the establishment of vineyards. Wine grapes often need warm days and cool nights, with minimal temperature extremes seasonally. Furthermore, ample sunlight, available soil nutrients, and sufficient water are required for grape production.

Due to variation in seasonal climates, growing and harvest conditions, and seasonal timing of production events, significant changes occur from year to year that make wines produced in certain years of higher or lower quality. Thus, the practice of labelling vintages of wine (the year of wine production) and the grape variety from which they were made is established so that enologists (people who study wine) can evaluate differences from year to year, as well as to ensure that enophiles (people who enjoy and collect wine) can purchase wines of known quality. Since many of the variables that go into wine production are not controllable by the wine producers, differences are bound to occur in each production cycle. The variation in wine flavors is therefore unending and the source of fascination for many who appreciate wine.

Beer

Among the oldest records of the production and use of alcoholic beverages is that of beer, which originated in Mesopotamia and the Babylonian regions of Asia at least fifty-five hundred years ago. Beer is a beverage obtained by fermenting carbohydrate-containing extracts of various grains with yeast. It is usually flavored with bittering substances to balance the sweet flavor of unfermented sugars, which are typically found in beer.

The brewing process begins by taking grains, usually barley (*Hordeum vulgare*), and producing malt. To do this, viable barley grains are steeped in water and allowed to germinate under controlled conditions. The germination process produces enzymes that begin to break down the complex carbohydrates (starch) found in the endosperm of the barley grains into soluble sugars.

When a specified stage of germination is reached, the enzyme concentration in the sprouted grains is maximised to an optimal level, and the entire process is halted abruptly by rapid drying (called kilning) of the grains to remove most of the water. At this stage the sprouted and dried grains are called malt. The degree of kilning of the malt determines the darkness and colour of the resulting beer; for instance, malts that are highly kilned produce beers with darker colour.

In order to extract a sufficient amount of fermentable sugars, the malt is crushed to expose the embryo and endosperm components; the ground malt is called grist. To begin conversion of starches and complex carbohydrates into fermentable sugars, the grist is mixed with water (the mash) and heated to a temperature of approximately 65°C (150°F). Under these conditions, the once active enzymes (amylases) are reactivated and continue to break down the carbohydrate materials. When the brewer determines that the conversion is complete, the fluid portions of the mash are removed through a process known as sparging, and the liquid (called sweet wort) is transferred to a boiling vessel.

The sweet wort is then boiled for a specific length of time, typically one to two hours, while the resinous, cone-like inflorescences of the hop plant (*Humulus lupulus;* family Cannabinaceae) are added to provide flavouring, aromatic, and bittering characteristics to the beer. Hops contain resins, collectively termed lupulin, which gives the beer its characteristic aroma and bitterness. Prior to the use of hops, other herbs, such as spruce, nettle, and woodruff were used for the same purpose: to balance the beer's sweetness with bitterness.

The boiling process also kills microorganisms that would otherwise spoil the wort, or produce undesirable fermentation products. The liquid that has been boiled with hops is now termed bitter wort; it is rapidly cooled and passed on to a fermentation vessel. Fermentation historically took place in open-topped fermenters, although modern commercial breweries use closed fermenters and are meticulous in their sanitary practices to ensure that fermentation is accomplished only by the yeast strain with which the brewer inoculates the cooled bitter wort.

Two main kinds of yeast are used: ales are beers fermented with beer strains of the yeast *Saccharomyces cerevisiae* at temperatures of 15° to 25°C (59° to 77°F); lagers are beers fermented with strains of *S. uvarum* at temperatures of 5° to 15°C (41° to 59°F), which are further conditioned (lagered) at near-freezing temperatures for several weeks or months. The alcohol content of the majority of beers is generally around 5 percent by volume, although certain styles of beer are produced with alcohol contents ranging from 8 to 14 percent and higher.

Some beers are naturally carbonated by continued slow fermentation after they are bottled, or they are artificially carbonated prior to bottling. Beers are also packaged in kegs (traditionally in oaken barrels) or in metal cans. Although the earliest beer production took place originally in the Middle East, the origins of modern beer styles can be traced to Germany, the United Kingdom, and the Czech Republic. There are a number of indigenous beers produced by many cultures around the world, but few have had as much influence on the brewing industry as those originating from the European region.

Spirits

Beverages produced from plant products that have been fermented and then distilled are considered spirits. The distillation process takes the fermented materials, often with a maximum alcohol content of 14 to 16 percent, and increases it to 40 to 75 percent alcohol by vaporizing the alcohol and many flavor components and then condensing them in specialised equipment known as stills. The concentrated alcoholic beverages resulting from this process are spirits or liquor, alluding to the condensate coming from the distillation process. Whiskeys (including Scotch or single-malt whiskey), bourbon, gin, vodka, rum, brandy, and various other liqueurs are produced through the distillation process.

Each begins with a different starting material prior to fermentation and these impart different flavor characteristics in the finished spirit. Spirits are measured for alcohol content, and are then described as having a certain proof, or twice the measured alcohol content (an 86 proof whiskey has an alcohol content of 43 percent, for example). Spirits are the major component of mixed drinks.

Other Alcoholic Beverages

A variety of other alcoholic beverages exist in nearly every culture. Often they are safer to drink than local water sources, which may contain parasites, so they are widely used. Additionally, many alcoholic beverages complement different cuisines of served foods, and in some cases have been shown to improve digestion. Sake is a beerlike beverage originating in Japan that uses rice as the source of carbohydrate materials and is double fermented using yeast and a species of *Aspergillus* fungus.

Cider (sometimes called hard cider) is an alcoholic beverage, popular in England, produced from yeast-fermented apple juice; it is occasionally flavored with a variety of spices. Mead, a beverage originating from medieval Europe, consists of honey that is fermented, occasionally together with other herbs or fruits, to produce a winelike drink that may be still or sparkling. The term "honeymoon" is coined from the practice of giving a gift of mead to a newly married couple: if they drank mead (honey) each night until the next moon, they would be given the gift of a new child.

Carbonated Drinks

Carbonated drinks continue to dominate the beverage market as opportunities arise to penetrate developing regions. However, there is a growing preference, especially among younger age groups, for health oriented alternatives, such as bottled water, fruit juices, energy, sports and "new age" drinks (such as iced tea). As a result, the number of product launches is increasing. New flavours and innovative packaging are being introduced to modify leading brands and extend their appeal. Based on this our beverage manufacturing customers are asking for:

— plant flexibility combined with productivity, to deliver high quality products at minimum cost of manufacture,
— production savings without compromising product quality.

2

Bar Management

During the past 20 years, bars have experienced a roller coaster of statistics. Although people still gather to socialise in bars, just as they have for hundreds of years, other factors have come into play for the industry as well. Problems with driving while intoxicated have changed the drinking patterns of people in all over the world. The growing concern with health and fitness toward the end of the 20th century took its toll on the bar industry. Keeping tabs on this industry requires a look at statistics of the alcoholic beverage industry as a whole—what people buy in the store doesn't differ much from what they buy in a bar.

Modern Alcoholic Beverage Industry

According to the Distilled Spirits Council of the United States, sales of distilled spirits declined considerably from 1980 to 1985 but turned around to a growth period in the late 1990s. Sales of white spirits (vodka, rum, gin and tequila) increased 0.6 percent from 1993 to 1997. They rose again from 1997 to 1998 1.6 percent. Sales of brown spirits, on the other hand, did the opposite, although the decline slowed in the late 1990s. From 1993 to 1997, sales of brown spirits dropped 3 percent and declined 1.5 percent from 1997 to 1998.

You can see how certain social issues have taken their toll on the sales of alcoholic beverages. Now let's take a look at the "state of the union," so to speak, for the United States bar industry as a whole. In the mid-1990s, the total number of operating liquor licenses in restaurants and bars exceeded 225,000 and beer and wine licenses reached more than half a million. Generally, the number of liquor licenses distributed is based on the population of the county.

In 1996, food and beverage workers held 4.6 million jobs, with 390,000 of those being bartenders. So what does all this mean to you? Well, it means you have some tough competition out there. But you're not just competing with the other bars in your area these days. You're competing with every entertainment option from which your customers can choose.

For Successful Bars

Successful new bars can be in the black within the first six months, and they can go on to recover their initial investment within three to five years. However, like many new businesses, the statistics aren't in favour of the startup. About 80 percent of new businesses fail within the first five years, and the bar business faces the same kind of statistics. Why do they fail? The first reason is they didn't have enough capital to keep the business going. The second reason is a lack of knowledge about the business.

From a personal perspective, you need to ask yourself if you're really the type of person who wants to own and run a bar. Of course, you don't have to run it if you own it, but you'd better make sure you have a team of good, trustworthy managers working for you if you plan to be "hands off." In the beginning, you will probably have to be greatly involved no matter whether or not you plan to be an active owner. If you're the kind of person who would rather deal with paperwork or sit in an office where you don't have to talk to people, this business is not for you. You will need to be out there talking to people and shaking hands. Getting to know your patrons, even if it's just to say "Hi" can go a long way for your customer service.

Another thing you should consider is the time commitment and time of day. If you're an early riser, you might not enjoy having to work until 3 or 4 a.m. at your bar. If you have a family, you need to discuss how owning a bar will affect them and your personal situation. Many times you will have to be at your bar from the time you wake up—say, around 10 or 11 a.m.—to the time you go to sleep—say, around 4 or 5 a.m.

As you can see, this could take its toll on your family life. Eventually, you'll probably be able to have a saner schedule, once your managers and staff are well-trained, but it may take six months to a year to reach that point. If this could cause problems for you or your family, you may want to reconsider the idea of owning a bar. From a business standpoint, however, a bar can provide an excellent return on investment.

Before you get started on the actual nuts and bolts of creating your dream bar, you have to decide what kind of establishment you'd like to own. Let's take a trip through the various kinds of bars—from neighbourhood bar to large-scale nightclub—and see which one is right for you.

Neighbourhood bar: Conceptually, the neighbourhood bar is still an American version of the English pub. You'll find them everywhere in the United States. If you own this kind of place, you can expect to know a great deal of your regular customers. As on the TV show "Cheers," you may find yourself taking phone messages for customers or cashing their paychecks. It's because of the friendly "home away from home" atmosphere that neighbourhood bars are successful. Some of these pubs open as early as 6 a.m., and they sometimes close earlier than other bars—depending on the clientele. This type of bar is perfect for small-scale entertainment options, such as darts, pool tables, video games and jukeboxes.

Across the country, this is probably the most popular type of bar you'll find. But there are a lot of neighbourhoods out there, so you might find that there is room for one more in your area. According to the experts the start-up cost for this kind of bar can range anywhere from $20,000 to $200,000, depending on the size and concept. The amount of revenue these businesses produce varies greatly depending on geographical location—big city or small town—and the size of the bar.

Sports bar. Depending on the establishment's capacity, sports bars can be a specific version of the neighbourhood tavern, or they can take on a life as big as a nightclub. You may have the latter in mind, but your market research may point to the former. It's important to do your homework!

Generally, sports bars offer some kind of menu options, such as sandwiches, burgers, pizza and appetizers. Since the main attraction is sporting events, sports bars have televisions in view of every seat, sometimes all tuned to different channels. Audio and video technology comes into play, with some owners spending a large percentage of their revenue on keeping up with the latest in technology—from satellites to big-screen TVs. The startup costs and revenue potential reflect basically the same numbers as a neighbourhood bar.

Brewpub or beer bar. Studies have shown that although consumers are drinking less alcohol, their tastes are becoming more discriminating. As a result, microbrews are becoming more and more popular. In a brewpub, you can brew your own beer right on the premises. In a beer bar, you can offer a large selection of different types of beer, including microbrews produced elsewhere. It's often easier to get a liquor license for a brewpub or beer bar than a full-scale liquor license since you don't need a fully stocked liquor bar.

Most brewpubs only sell their own beer options on tap (draft beer), with a few selections of bottled beer options, too. Since you're creating your own product in a brewpub, you also have the ability to control what you make and sell—from quality to quantity. The startup costs of a brewpub can be quite high—from $100,000 to $1 million—because of the brewing equipment you need to have. If you produce a popular beer, you have the opportunity to grow into a very successful operation to make two or three times your startup costs.

Beer bars tend to have lower startup costs, which can often mean obtaining a less expensive, fixed-price license from your state government. Beer bar startup costs range from about $20,000 to $100,000, depending on size and location. The revenue potential depends on the geographical location and drinking trends in the community.

Wine and champagne bar: This kind of bar often gives guests the opportunity to taste a variety of different kinds of wines and the ability to learn more about their qualities. Wine and champagne bars tend to stay small and intimate in size and are located in more sophisticated neighbourhoods.

Again, because you only need a beer and wine license to open this type of bar, your licensing fees drop considerably. Depending on the type of product you serve and the extent of your decor, you can expect to find the cost and revenues close to the amounts for a beer bar.

Nightclub: Like the neighbourhood bar, nightclubs can take on a number of different personalities. You can open a small "cocktail lounge" with a jukebox or a tinkling piano in the corner. A medium-sized nightclub might look like a neighbourhood bar during the lunchtime hours, then spring to life with a popular band at night. Or if you have a big enough budget, your nightclub might be a large dance club where the most fashionable people and hippest celebrities hang out every weekend. Whichever path you take, you must be prepared to spend a great deal of time and money on promotion to create your "buzz." Nightclubs can make plenty of money if they're managed properly.

As a bar owner, you need to embark on the same kind of relentless detective work to profile your customers before you start investing large sums of money in your business. The majority of the research material you need is probably already available to you. You simply have to compile it. You can go about developing your customer profile in several different ways, then compare the results to determine your direction.

— *General demographics*: Your bar's concept may go in a totally different direction if you're in a college town with a high percentage of young, single students than if you're in a quiet, conservative suburb populated with families.

— *Alcohol trends*: National and regional alcohol suppliers keep records of how their product fits into the market. Your potential suppliers can provide valuable information about your customers and what they like to drink. Generally, they are glad to help. If you do your research and have a successful bar, your suppliers will profit, too.

— *Other important statistics*: Visit your local public library or university library. Many libraries have business departments that have a wealth of information about demographics, income levels and spending trends.

— *Lifestyle trends*: Call the lifestyle and entertainment editors at your local newspaper and regional magazines, as well as the advertising and marketing departments of local radio stations. They can give you information about your competitors and tell you more about the establishments that have been successful in the area.

— *Your customers and the competition:* You can discover a ton of information about your customers using internet resources. Besides general demographics, you can surf the web for information about other bars in the area. Pop into chat areas and newsgroups to find out where the action is and which bars are the hot spots.

Using Your Research

Once you've compiled all your research, you can devise a concrete profile of your clientele. For example, you may decide your target customers are professionals between the ages of 30 and 50 who have incomes of more than $35,000 and like jazz music. Whatever you set as your target market will affect all the decisions you make from here on, so make sure you get it right!

Once you have your profile, you can develop your menu and bar inventory based on what customers like. Look for trade magazines and industry associations that provide data on food and beverage spending patterns. Keep in mind that you may have more than one profile to work with. You may have a conservative professional clientele during the daytime and a rowdy college crowd at night. If you use your research wisely, you can develop a bar that caters to both profiles for even more business.

The bar/tavern industry can be a pricey undertaking. Because of the high failure rate, you may come across desperate bar owners willing to take a low purchase price just to get out of the business. You'll also find that startup costs for bars vary depending on size, location and target market.

Your bar's size, location, type and concept will make your startup cost as individual as your business. Again, you could buy an existing bar that would nullify all the numbers on our low-end chart, or start a large-scale nightclub that's off the map from our high-end numbers. You'll have to do some research to find out what your bar will cost based on your concept, size and location.

The groundwork you lay to operate your bar includes the systems you use to track liquor and food. How much does the customer owe the server/bartender, and in turn, how much do they owe you? Also, what liquor and food do you sell the most? The systems you choose depend on the type and size of bar you have.

In most bars, only the bartenders and servers handle money. Cashiers or takeout staff may also have cash-handling responsibilities. Factors to consider when choosing an accounting system include the level of sales you expect, both from alcohol and food, and the efficiency needed for your staff to operate at its full potential. Also, look for holes that your accounting system might leave open for theft at all levels, not just servers and bartenders. No one thinks they are hiring a thief. Many people who might steal if the opportunity arose do not consider themselves thieves, either, so they don't come off as such.

If you use the cash-and-carry system, where the drink is ordered by the server verbally and then paid for before the bartender or server rings it up, you might find many "forgot to ring it up" drinks, as well as a few given away for free. It is the nature of the system. If your inventory controls are so tight that you will notice when too much has been used, or if your manager, who shares in the profits anyway, is your bartender, then you can use this system without much fear.

Perfect Location

Your choice of location will depend on how you want your bar to look, what you want your bar to contribute to the community, and the kind of clientele you want to patronise it. Then you need to decide whether you want to buy the location or sign a lease. Again, that depends on your budget. Finally, you need to figure out how to fuse your concept with both your name and your location to your best advantage.

People who know this industry well have polar opinions on the concept of location. Some owners and experts put enormous importance on the bar's location while others refuted its significance altogether. It all depends on what you want your bar to be and what your strengths are as an owner. If you want your bar to get impulsive neighbourhood traffic in a particular area, then you should be closest, and most obvious, to them.

If you'd rather spend the time and money, saved by more affordable real estate, to develop your establishment's concept and create your own buzz and destination, your actual location won't matter so much. You should consider factors such as safety, parking, accessibility to customers—even the history of the site—when choosing a location.

The word "location" can refer to two different things—what area your bar is in (downtown, uptown, suburbs, etc.) and where you are in relation to your customers. Are you on their way home from work? Or do they have to make it a point to get to you? Michael O'Harro, a National Bar & Restaurant Management Association board member, explains how he took a bar location nobody wanted in Virginia and made it work.

"It was in an alley," he says. "It was a 15-foot-wide alley, and we were 128 feet away from the street. No one would go up the alley—[people] were afraid of it. So the building sat empty for 50 years. But the bar at the end of the alley was spending $20,000 a month in rent, while my rent was $500.

Naming

When it comes to naming a bar, experts generally fall into two major schools of thought. The first says your bar is your dream—your hard work—so you should name it anything you want. The second approach to naming says your moniker is the first and greatest form of advertising for your drinking establishment.

Now that you have your entertainment in place and ready to go, it's time to start planning how you're going to get people into your bar to enjoy it. Just like any other aspect of operating your bar, marketing is an ongoing process. Many bar owners think marketing is the most fun and exciting aspect of running a bar.

There are still ways to get some advertising and marketing out there without spending a ton of money. But anytime you reach into your own pocket to buy advertising for a bar, it's not good. Your employees love working there. They are talking and saying great things about the place, and that is passed on to your customers. The customers love being there, and they tell other customers. If you can get to that point, it's just priceless." You can create special promotions for your bar, launch a direct-mail campaign with a newsletter for regular customers, develop a web site, and any other creative marketing techniques you can dream up.

Promotional Events

After you bar is up and running, you'll have a better idea

of what nights need a little boost. Most bars are busy on Friday and Saturday nights, with Thursdays coming in third place. You might decide you need to pump up business on Monday or Tuesday, so pick one day and keep it going until you have established enough regular business to move the promotions to a different day. Here are some ideas to keep in mind when you're working on promotional events.

— *Prepare*: Work out a budget. If your promotion continues for more than one day, budget for the entire time you want it to run. A good goal to shoot for is to make a profit that's three times the cost of the promotion.

— *Make a schedule*: Design a planning calendar at least eight weeks before the promotion. Depending on the size and magnitude of the promotion, you may want to start advertising it at this point, too. Never advertise an ending date, though, so you can cut it early if it doesn't do as well as you planned, or you can extend it if it really takes off.

— *Maintain the energy level*: On the day of the promotion, don't stop the action to give away prizes or make announcements. You can turn the music down, but don't turn it off. This will keep the energy level high and consistent. If you absolutely have to turn off the music, never keep it off for more than 10 minutes, or you risk people getting impatient and leaving.

— *Party all night*: Schedule your prize giveaways, contests and entertainment to run throughout the night. If you have a grand prize to give away or a finale planned, don't do it until after midnight so your guests stay in your bar as late as possible.

Promoting your bar can be fun and creative. During a promotion and after it's over, ask your customers and your employees for feedback and critiques. Of course, your sales will give you a lot of the information you're looking for, too.

Planning the Profit

Alcohol sales (beverage sales) are an easy way to increase profitability because the costs are lower and the gross margin is far greater for beverage than for food. However, beverage costs must be controlled if an operation is to reach maximum potential of gross profit from beverage sales. Every reduction in beverage cost percentage renders a higher gross profit. Beverage costs that are above industry averages can negatively impact your profitability.

A profitable restaurant typically generates a 22% to 28% beverage cost. Because of the impact beverage costs can make on an operation, it is important to know where beverage cost falls in relation to total sales on a daily or weekly basis. Beyond the bottom line, beverage costs also reflect an operation's control systems, management skill level, and value provided to the customers.

Many restaurant managers do not calculate beverage cost correctly, or if they do, they do not fully understand the process. If calculated correctly, the ratio can be compared to industry averages and previous performance. Alcoholic beverages are included in beverage cost calculations. Soft drinks, juices, coffees, and other non-alcoholic beverage sales are included in food cost calculations.

With an accurate beverage cost, steps can be taken to improve the operation and ultimately improve the bottom line. The following is a step-by-step method for calculating beverage cost including an example and a worksheet to calculate your own beverage cost.

Keeping in mind that eventually you want to compare your beverage cost with industry averages, how you determine the numbers must be consistent with industry practices. The industry standard is based on the Uniform System of Accounts for Restaurants. This system clearly identifies what items are included in each part of the beverage cost formula and is briefly outlined below.

Beverage Cost = Cost of Beverage Sales / Total Beverage Sales

The beverage sales and costs should be generated during a set accounting time period of at least two weeks or more typically, every 28 days, or monthly. Soft drinks, juices, coffee, and other non-alcoholic beverage sales are included in *food* cost calculations, not beverage cost calculations.

Time Frame

Working with your accountant and managers, set up a regular time frame to analyse beverage cost. It is critical that the elements of the beverage cost calculation (sales, inventories and purchases) are representative of this time period.

Beverage Sales

This is the relatively easy part—total the customer checks or reports from point-of-sale registers—making sure to only include sales generated from beverage sources (sources other than beverage should be allocated to a "food" or "other income" account). Remember to use sales generated only within the allotted time frame.

Cost of beverage sales

The costs associated with beverage sales are comprised of *purchases* and *inventory level adjustments*. In our experience, this part of the calculation is often computed incorrectly.

Equally important, and often not included in determining cost of beverage sales, is the inventory adjustment. Many restaurants consider only purchases in determining beverage cost. This does not create an accurate beverage cost percentage—depending on the day purchases are made and what the cut-off date is for including sales in the beverage cost calculation, your beverage cost could appear higher or lower than it actually is. Additionally, this discrepancy makes it difficult to compare and track beverage costs.

For example, suppose you receive (purchase) all your spirits and wine products on Thursday to prepare for the weekend. The time period for determining beverage cost ends on Friday (the next day). In calculating your beverage cost, it appears much higher than last month. While the increase may be due to theft or another operational issue, most likely it is due to calculating your beverage cost inconsistently and incorrectly. Your purchases reflect a large Thursday delivery, however, you do not log the sales from the weekend to offset these purchases, making your beverage cost appear out of line. Additionally, you have not factored in the inventory adjustment.

Determine Physical Inventory

To properly determine beverage cost, a physical inventory of the main bar, service bar and storeroom areas must be conducted at the end of each period. Once you have your ending period inventory level, look at the *change* from your beginning (start of time period) inventories (bars and storerooms). The key to accurate cost determination is understanding the role inventory levels play. For example, if the beginning inventory level is valued at $100 and four weeks later the ending inventory for the period is valued at $75, the inventory adjustment is the $25 difference—an increase in cost of beverage sales because you used $25 worth of inventory and did not replace it with new purchases.

Considering this change and its effect on cost of beverage sales, apply the difference to the total purchases for the time period, giving you the total cost of beverage sales.

Cost of Beverage Sales =Purchases+/- Inventory Adjustment

Successful restaurants generate beverage costs in the mid 20% range. However, different types of operations typically run higher or lower percentages—fine dining may run up to 35% (sales of bottles of wine are usually less profitable other alcoholic beverages) whereas brewpub restaurants may run about 15%. Comparing your cost percentage to restaurants with similar menus and service levels provides a more accurate perspective.

The 1997 RAS Report is a restaurant operations report for Pennsylvania restaurants which provides industry information and food and beverage cost averages based on menu-theme, sales volume, years in business and other categories. For example, the report lists an average beverage cost of 32.1% for American/Regional menu themed restaurants and 30.8% for a restaurant in a multi-unit organisation.

The next step requires compiling the sales and costs consistently and regularly, as comparisons to previous performance can prove very helpful, identifying problems and trends—remembering that a *decrease* in beverage cost is as important to investigate as an increase. From here, your operation is positioned to tighten its beverage cost by looking closely at various methods used to control beverage cost—with the ultimate goal of positively impacting your bottom line.

Controlling the Cost

There are many methods used to control liquor costs and every operator needs to determine which methods should be implemented. The following are some basic methods that could be applied. A combination of several different controls is the best way to ensure tight control and therefore see the maximum potential liquor sales offer.

Par Stocked Bar

— The bar should be stocked based on a number of bottles of each brand sold on the busiest day plus a margin for safety.

— Bottles should only be restocked by managers and only on a bottle for bottle basis.

Receiving and storing

— Purchasing and receiving functions should be undertaken by separate individuais. The beverage buyer should not be the same person receiving the merchandise. A receiving report is generated by the purchasing manager stating the quantities, sizes, and agreed upon prices for the order. The receiver is responsible for inspecting the order when it comes in and making sure it matches the report.

— All bottles received should be marked in a way that makes the bottle identifiable as a house bottle (to prevent bartenders from bringing in their own bottles and keeping the profits)

— All received merchandise should then be stored in a locked area where access is limited to as few people as possible (ideally just one), as this allows shortages to be traced.

Maintenance

— A perpetual inventory should be maintained for each time period with adjustments for purchases and requisitions. This perpetual inventory should be compared against a physical inventory at the close of every period and variances should be noted and investigated.

Bartending Standards

— All bartenders should be required to complete all transactions for sales immediately, either by opening a tab or accepting payment. Any delay in this makes it easier to "forget" to ring in a sale.
— Some method of recording sales should be employed in a consistent way. Either red lining a dupe once payment is made or filing copied dupes for each shift.
— An accurate pouring method should be utilised.
— Drink recipes should be consistent and readily available.

These methods of control and properly calculating your beverage cost will go a long way in assisting you, the restaurateur, to manage beverage costs and increase profitability.

3

Brandy

Brandy is a liquor distilled from wine (brandy) or fermented fruit juice (fruit brandy). Is is then are aged in wood containers, which contributes flavor and color. The name "brandy" comes from the Dutch *brandewijn*, meaning "burned wine".

History of Brandy

Some historians credit the Chinese with discovering the art of turning fruit wine or grain-based mash into a higher alcohol, purer beverage. Others claim the Egyptians were the creators of distillation. It's possible that both cultures were both experimenting with distillation in roughly the same period. Whatever the case, we know for certain that the Moors first established distillation in Europe during their occupation of southern Spain from the 8th century to the late 15th century.

The Spaniards of the period were skilled winemakers and started using the pot stills that were left behind by the Moors. Within a century, brandies made from fermented grapes and other fruits spread across continental Europe. "Brandy" is derived from brandywijn, a word of Dutch origin for "burnt". Created in a still to leave the water and remove the alcoholic vapour which condenses back into liquid form as it cools. In other languages too, it is the burning that is the essential feature.

In theory distillation is the simplest of physical processes. It is based on the fact that alcohol and water boil at different temperatures, water at 100°C, alcohol at 78.3°C. If a fermented liquid is heated, the vapour containing the alcoholic constituents is released first. It can then be trapped and cooled, then condensed to an alcoholic liquid.

The process was probably first observed by the Arabs, who carried the torch of science during the Dark Ages. We still use their words "al-ambiq" (alembic) for the still, "al-kuhl" (alcohol) for the distillate. Originally, the object was to produce medicinal properties, but it was soon discovered that the use of an appropriate raw material produced a drinkable liquid, a "water of life", aqua vitae.

But the raw materials were generally so impure that the alcohol could only be consumed with safety if it had been repeatedly redistilled, which removed most of the essential characteristics of the original raw material as well. The biggest breakthrough came in the 16th and early 17th centuries when it was found that distilling the sharp white wines, produced on the slopes overlooking the little town of Cognac in western France, resulted in spirits which, after as few as two passes through the stills, produced an eminently drinkable brandy, especially if aged for a few years in oak casks. It has proved to be an unbeatable formula.

The next essential in making fine brandy is the speed of distillation: the slower, the gentler, the more effectively the aromatic elements in the raw material are detached with the alcohol, the better. It is rather like stewing fruit: the lower the flame on the stove, the more intense the aromas released and the more thoroughly is the residue drained of them. Indeed, the Cognacais like to describe their method of distillation as (speeded-up) evaporation. They are right: the vapours should contain as high a proportion as possible of the congeners, the hundreds of organic chemical compounds which are extracted with the alcohol.

Some of these are undesirable, bringing with them rank and unpleasant aromas and have to be removed. This entails a close control over the distillation process to remove the "heads", the first vapours emerging from the still, which contain the bulk of these undesirable elements, and then the "tails" which will simply be too feeble, without the requisite alcoholic concentration. At the other extreme are the continuous stills, invented early in the 19th century by, and named after, an Irishman, Coffey. This still can concentrate wine 10 or more times up to the normal industrial maximum of 96.6%.

This fast, continuous process saves heat (pot-stills have to be reheated between each batch), is highly productive - and can be highly destructive of all the elements which make brandy interesting. Newly distilled brandy tastes raw, oily and unappetizing. The key to its final quality is a more or less lengthy sojourn in oak casks. The choice of wood was originally accidental: oak happened to be the most easily available for making the casks required by the pioneering distillers. They were, of course, accustomed to using wood to mature and market their wines.

Because brandy, like wine, is a product of the grape, oak has proved suitable for maturing it. But there are many varieties of oak and as with so many aspects of brandy making, local practices differ so widely that only a few generalisations can be offered as applying to the whole range of brandies. Most of the qualities which make oak so suitable are physical.

For whatever the chemical qualities of the wood and the reactions they induce when in prolonged contact with the spirit, it is the porosity of the cask which allows the brandy to have a steady, limited access to the air. The brandy gradually absorbs the oxygen required to oxidise and thus soften the raw spirit.

Wine Brandies

The best known of all wine based brandies is the French Cognac produced in the Cognac (Charente) region of France. A relative of the Cognac is the Armagnac. It has a richer taste but less finesse than the Cognac. Several other countries than France produce brandies. Some of them are Spain, Portugal, Italy, Greece, Germany, the United States, Chile and Peru.

Spanish Brandy

The Spanish brandies are a by-product of the production of sherry. They have a full flavor and are slightly sweet.

Greek Brandy

One famous Greek brandy is the Metaxa. It is distilled from red grapes, sweetened and flavored with herbs.

South American brandy

The best known South American brandy is the Pisco, national drink of Chile.

Brandy is not always distilled from the wine. Marc, from France, and grappa, from Italy, are distilled from the remaining skins, husks and stems of the wine production. They are not always aged and have a light yellow color (if any).

Fruit Brandies

Most fruit brandies are made from fermented fruit mash (such as apples and pears), but other sugar-poor fruits not capable of fermentation (such as raspberries and blackberries) can be soaked in neutral spirits and then re-distilled. Most fruit brandies are aged in steel, glass or clay containers, keeping them colorless and clear. Within the general category of fruit brandies, a distinction is made between distillates from pomaceous fruits, stone fruits and berries.

Pomaceous fruits brandy

This is fruit brandy made from apple and pear. A must or cider is made from the fruit, aged and then distilled. This produce a raw distillate with high alcohol content. The distillate is then diluted with water and sometimes aged on casks. The best known apple brandy is Calvados.

Brandy from stone fruits

The most important stone-fruit brandy is kirschwasser made from sweet or sour cherries. Other popular stone-fruit brandies are plum brandy and apricot brandy.

Brandy from berries

Most berries have too little fruits to ferment properly, and are soaked in neutral spirits which absorbs the flavors. The alcohol and berries is then distilled. The best known berry-brandy is the raspberry brandy, but brandies are also made from bilberries, blackberries, strawberries, black and red currant and cranberries.

Fruit brandies are either served neat as an aperitif or used in mixed drinks. Fruit brandy served neat should not be chilled.

Most cognoscenti think of Cognac when the word brandy is mentioned. While the word brandy captures all wine distillates. Each country, each region and even each distillery strives to achieve a unique style. Since grape flavour and aroma change pending on terroir, the resultant distillate of each wine ends up with a distinct flavour to which the type of still and aging add additional taste dimensions.The Charantais (inhabitants of Charante Maritime, the department of origin of Cognac) were able to sell their brandy first to the Dutch and then to the British navy merchants in the 16th century who in turn marketed it world wide. Undeniably, most Cognac are fine, refined and elegant products mainly due to the terroir, production techniques, care in aging, and expertise in blending.

Packaging and marketing savvy contribute greatly to world-wide success. But Armagnac, from Gascony, also in France and located just south of Bordeaux pleases millions with its deep spicy and rustic flavours. It is an excellent brandy to enjoy, particularly after a rich meal, but you can also mix it with water to enjoy as an aperitif or even in cocktails/ Armagnac differs from Cognac in the grape varieties used, teroir and distilling techniques. Also, Armagnac is aged in Gascony oak barrels, versus Limousin or Troncais oak barriques for Cognac. If you like brandy, Armagnac might please you particularly if you taste V S O P, X O or reserve personelle- quality products.

Other French regions produce brandy as well but most are either exported in bulk to be blended, or purchased by distillers within the country and blended. Some are good, even fine, at a fraction of the cost of Cognac or Armagnac, but they lack refinement in texture, depth in taste, and smoothness in the finish.

Spain

Today the majority of Jerez brandy base wine originates

in La Mancha, in the heart of Spain. The base grape is Airen, the most widely planted white grape on earth, brandies must be aged and blended in the region. Some producers (most if not all are sherry bodegas) even use soleras to age and blend. The minimum aging period is three years but most are matured for more than 10 years and can be truly great. Some may contain a little more caramel than a few connoisseurs might like, but in general they are respectable brandies. Some are Llepanto, Cardenal Mendoza, Carlos I, Gran Duque d'Alba, Conde de Osborne and Lustau.

Portugal

Portuguese bagaciera tend to be harsh, fiery, and spicy. They cost little, and if consumed with soft drinks or in cocktails, are fine.

Italy

Best known for good-quality brandies like Branca, Oro Pilla and Stock (X O aged for nine years) Italy also boasts some small distillers like Buton famous for its Vecchia Romagna brands. The distillery employs both pot- and continuous stills and ages the distillates separately which are blended prior to bottling, Buton's Vecchia Romagna Etichetta Nera (Black Label) is a blend of three year old pot – and continuous still brandies, whereas Oro (Gold Label) contains seven year old components. Buton has also extra old (25 and 35 year old) brandies marketed in very small quantities and specially designed bottles.

Villa Zari, a small Tuscan distiller uses Trebbiano grapes grown on Chianti Hills Only free run juice wine is used for extra finesse. After an initial nine month, small new oak aging, the brandy is transferred to even smaller but older barrels to avoid excessive tannin absorption.

Germany

Germans consume substantial quantities of brandy and produce considerable amounts. Even then, base wine and/ or finished product must be imported, mostly from France and/or Italy for aging and blending. Asbach Uralt, and Dujardin are two most famous brands. Both companies export to other European countries and North America. German brandies are light, fragrant and well-aged products with a fine balance. They can be enjoyed on their own, in cocktails and with soft drinks.

Greece

Greeks have been associated with winemaking for more than 2000 years however distillation seems to have been an after thought.

Sypros Metaxa was the first to distil wine in 1888 and the company he founded now sells over a million cases world wide. Metaxa is double-distilled and aged for variable lengths of time pending the quality of end product desired. The company markets three to seven year old aged brandies distinguished by stars, each of which represents one year of aging. Metaxa adds a little Muscat wine for smoothness and extra aroma.

Extra old Metaxa brandies are marketed in handsome, painted, ceramic bottles. Tirnavou is the other export-oriented Greek distiller with fine brands. Greek brandies have gained world-wide popularity with considerable help from Greek restaurateurs in North America, northern European countries and Australia, and sun-starved northern European tourists visiting this sunny Mediterranean country.

Cyprus

On the Greek section of Cyprus, the wine growing

Haggipavlou family imported a pot still from Cognac in 1868 that is still operational Brandy is popular among Cypriots and some even drink it throughout their meals. Anglias, the first blended brandy of Cyprus (1930), is the most popular both in the country and Cypriot brandy exported to the U. K. Cypriot brandies are well made and deeply flavoured with a sweetish tinge but a pleasant and lingering aftertaste many associate with quality.

Turkey

Turkey produces significant amounts of grapes, most of which are fine for our-of-hand eating. Yet a portion ends up as wine and also as brandy called Kanyak. Distilling is a government monopoly and quality takes a backseat to quantity. Turkish brandy tends to be light, harsh, and generally insipid.

Israel

Israel is the largest kosher brandy producer in the world. The first still was shipped from France, by the wine-branch of the Rothschild family. Kosher brandy must be distilled from kosher wine subject to many rules and regulations. The vines must be at least three years old, grapes hand-harvested. Rotten grapes must be discarded prior to pressing. All musts must be fermented with ndigenous yeast and the wine must be made in extra cle: n premises employing kosher-keeping individuals. All kosher vineyards fruit must be sold to gentiles every seventh year. Kosher bandies of Israel tend to have a sweetish edge preferred by locals.

France, Italy and the U S A also produce kosher brandy. In fact some mashgiachs (religious supervisors) accept all distilled products as kosher so long the distillery is known to follow strict hygienic rules and regulations.

Armenia

Armenian brandy has always been the preferred distillate of USSR diplomats. The Yerevan Brandy factory, in the capital of this tiny republic in the Caucasus mountains, is now owned and managed by Pernod Ricard, a huge French beverage alcohol conglomerate. Yerevan Brandy Factory markets its products under the Ararat brand available in three, five, eight, 12, and 18 year old, all of which are aged in oak barrels of Krasnoyarsk oak. The young (three to five year old,) brandies tend to be somewhat rough on the edges, but those eight, 12 and 18 year old exude fine apricot and vanilla aromas much appreciated by connoisseurs and others alike.

Texturally Armenian brandies trend to be refined, light and smooth. Packaging has been improved and Pernod-Ricard instituted ambitious export campaigns to increase volume. Most Armenian brandy is exported to Russia and a little to western countries.

Georgia

Georgia, located just north of Armenia, has been distilling brandy for centuries. They tend to be flavourful, but display a rustic texture mostly due to short aging in inappropriate casks and limited blending expertise.

South Africa

Brandy is the national South African distillate mostly produces for the mass-market palate by KWV, however this huge winery-cum-distillery markets also a 10 year old well blended international-award-winning brandies at extremely attractive prices.

Boplaas, in the Klein Karoo issue a five year old Colombard brandy, whereas Clos Cabriere uses Chardonnay, and Paarl Rock Muscat d'Alexandrie, and

Backberg Chenin Blanc. South African distillers make and market a wide range of appealing brandies well worth looking for.

Australia

Australian brandies can be quite pleasant, but much of it is consumed within the country. Brandy has been distilled and aged in Australia for long time, but only recently have some producers attempted to export.

Mexico

Contrary to wide-held belief, Mexicans prefer brandy over tequila and other distillates. Presidente and Don Pedro are the largest selling brandies in the world (5.8 and 3.5 million cases respectively). Both brands are sweetened with syrup but solera aged and blended. Mexicans like to drink their brandy on the rocks with Coca Cola.

USA

Although brandy has been distilled and aged in California since mid 1800's for the most part Americans treated them as second class products. Most were used in cocktails, such as brandy Alexander, Sidecars, Brandy and coke and cooking. With the relatively recent explosion of California wine profile. Connoisseurs are starting to take a second look at American brandy, realising their unique taste and smoothness.

Korbel, Christian Brothers, P. Masson's Grande Amber, and E and J Gallo's E and J are market leaders. Recently small, quality-oriented batch distillers such as Germain Robin, R M S Distillery (both in California) and Dry Creek Distillery in Oregon have been gaining market share. All cater to a small, sophisticated niche markets that value quality over price. RMS, located in Carneros

(Sonoma) and Germain Robin in Mendocino county, stand out with fragrant, smooth and light brandies much in favour today. Both use a range of grape varieties including Colombard, Chenin Blanc, Pinot Noir, Palomino, Muscat, Folle Blanche, Viognier, Chardonnay and Semillon.

RMS's QE (Quality Extraordinaire) consists of six brandies derived from Chenin Blanc, Palomino, Muscat, Ugni Blanc and Folle Blanche). The fruit is picked at low Brix levels in an attempt to obtain enough acidity, which ultimately ends up rendering the end-product light, fragrant and very appealing.

Germain Robin uses Charantais alembics (a tulip shaped still with a swan neck, hand-made from thick copper) for a rare Pinot Noir brandy using 12 different grape brandies, and X O aged in Limousine oak barrels. Both are of outstanding quality, clarity, smoothness and fragrance. While high quality American brandies are distilled in French alembic-style stills, large plants like Jepson in Ukiah, prefer efficient continuous Coffey stills (Columnar stills, named after an Irish liquor inspector stationed in Scotland and who invented the device) that triple-distill in one process. Clear Creek Distillery in Portland, Oregon and St George Spirits in Alameda concentrate on fruit brandies, but also produce some grape brandies of high quality.

American brandy producers prefer Limousin oak barrels for aging although Rupf, owner of St George Distillery swears by Nevers oak from Burgundy and believes his Chardonnay brandy to taste as good, if not better, than nay in Cognac and/or Armagnac. All American brandy distillers have come to the conclusion that aging and blending constitute the most important processes, a fact their French counterparts had discovered centuries ago. All age their varietal brandies separately and blend to achieve balance, elegance, smoothness, fine bouquet and depth of flavours. Pinot Noir provides complexity and depth, Colombard freshness, Palomino muskiness, Chenin Blanc nutiness, Semillon fruitiness, Sauvignon Blanc exotic, grassy flavours and delicacy along with floral tones. Fine American brandies tend to be as refined as any from Jerez, Cognac, Armagnac or Germany.

Canada

Canada's Kittling Ridge, in Grimsby, Ontario is well-known for its Ontario small cask oak-aged brandy that exudes stone fruit aromas, possesses a refined texture and lightness few other brandies can hope to achieve. Cheminaud, Barclay, D'Eaubonne are other blended brandies from local and imported base material Brandy, in particular Cognac, has been very popular in Hong Kong but when the city started losing financial clout after it was taken over by China, and due to the 1997 recession its importance has suffered among Cognac exports.

However, Cognac exporters have been able to open two other lucrative Asian markets: Taiwan and Japan. Brandy has been the preferred distillate of millions for centuries, and is likely to stay that way, even though its popularity may have suffered somewhat lately!

4

DISTILLED SPIRITS

A distilled beverage, also called spirits, is a preparation for consumption containing ethyl alcohol purified by distillation, or other method, from a substance such as wine, grain or wood. It is any alcohol mixture 15 percent or higher. The term is usually restricted to alcoholic beverages.

Beer and wine are limited to a maximum 15 percent alcohol, beyond which yeast is adversely affected and can not ferment. Higher levels of alcohol have historically been obtained in a number of ways. Wine heated in an animal bladder draws out water and leaves alcohol behind (the bladder has a natural property which removes water), but there is no evidence this method was used before modern times.

Another method, called freeze distillation, involves freezing the alcoholic beverage and removing water crystals, a method which has been known to have been in use in central Asia, known as the "Mongolian still", as early as the 7th century. In Europe and North America, this method was used to make applejack from cider. However the freezing method had limitations in geography and implementation and thus did not have widespread use. This leaves the method of distillation from which most of the history of distilled beverages is drawn.

History of Distillation

In a basic form the technique of distillation goes back to Babylonia in the fourth millennium BC when specially shaped clay plots, it is thought, were used to extract some small amounts of distilled alcohol through natural cooling, for the manufacture of perfumes. It is unlikely this device ever played a meaningful role in the history of the development of the still. Distillation seems to have been known by alchemists in Alexandria, around the 3rd century AD, who used alcohol only for the coloring of metal and sublimation and was not widely known.

The development of the still with cooled collector — necessary for the distillation of spirits — was an invention of Islamic alchemists in the 8th or 9th centuries. In particular, Geber invented the alembic still, from which he observed heated wine released a flammable vapor, which he described as "of little use, but of great importance to science". Not much later Al-Razi (864–930) described the distillation of alcohol and its use in medicine.

By that time, distilled spirits were not just chemical products, but fairly popular beverages: the poet Abu Nuwas describes a wine that "has the color of rain-water but is as hot inside the ribs as a burning firebrand". The terms "alembic" and "alcohol", and possibly the metaphors "spirit" and *acqua vitæ* ("life-water") for the distilled product, can be traced to Islamic alchemy.

The practice of calling distilled alcoholic beverages for "life-water" has given the name to several types of beverages, like gaelic whisky, french eaux-de-vie and possibly vodka. Also, the scandinavian akvavit spirit gets its name from the latin phrase *Aqua vitae*.

Alcohol appears first in Europe in the mid 12th century among alchemists, who were more interested in medical "elixirs" than making gold from lead. It first appears under the name *aqua ardens* (burning water) in the *Compendium Salerni* from the medical school at Salerno. The recipe was written in code suggesting it was kept a secret. Taddeo Alderotti in his *Consilia medicinalis* refers to the "serpente" which is believed to have been the coiled tube of a still.

Paracelsus gave alcohol its modern name, taking it from the Arabic word which means "finely divided", in reference to what is done to wine. His test was to burn a spoonful without leaving any residue. Other ways of testing were to burn a cloth soaked in it without actually harming the cloth. In both cases to achieve this effect the alcohol had to have been at least 95 percent.

Claims on the origins of alcoholic beverages are controversial, often invoking national pride, but they are plausible after the 12th century when Irish whiskey, German Hausbrand and German Brandy can all be safely said to have arrived. These beverages would have had much lower alcohol content, around 40 percent, and had "universal" medicinal elixir application.

After the mid 14th century, when distilled liquors were commonly applied as remedies for the Black Death, consumption of liquor rose dramatically in Europe. Around 1400 it was discovered how to distill spirits from beer and grain spirits (corn, barley, rye) and even sawdust was used to make alcohol, a much cheaper option than grapes. Thus began the "national" drinks of Europe: jenever (Belgium and the Netherlands), gin (England), schnapps (Germany), aquavit (Scandinavia), vodka (Russia). The actual names only emerged in the 16th century but the drinks were well known .

The distilled spirits industry includes the production of whisky, gin, vodka, rum, and brandy. Distilled spirits production also may include the production of secondary products such as distillers dried grains used for livestock feed and other feed/food components.

Distilled spirits, including grain spirits and neutral spirits, are produced throughout the United States. The Bureau of Alcohol, Tobacco, and Firearms (BATF) has established "standards of identity" for distilled spirits products.

Production Process

Distilled spirits can be produced by a variety of processes. Typically, in whisky production, grains are mashed and fermented to produce an alcohol/water solution, that is distilled to concentrate the alcohol. For whiskies, the distilled product is aged to provide flavor, color, and aroma. Figure 1 is a simple diagram of a typical whisky production process. Emission data are available only for the fermentation and aging steps of whisky production.

Handling Grains

Distilleries utilise premium cereal grains, such as hybrid corn, rye, barley, and wheat, to produce the various types of whisky and other distilled spirits. Grain is received at a distillery from a grainhandling facility and is prepared for fermentation by milling or by malting (soaking the grains to induce germination). All U.S. distillers purchase malted grain instead of performing the malting process onsite.

Grain Mashing

Mashing consists of cooking the grain to solubilise the starch from the kernels and to convert the soluble starch to grain sugars with barley malt and/or enzymes. Small quantities of malted barley are sometimes added prior to grain cooking. The mash then passes through a noncontact cooler to cool the converted mash prior to entering the fermenter.

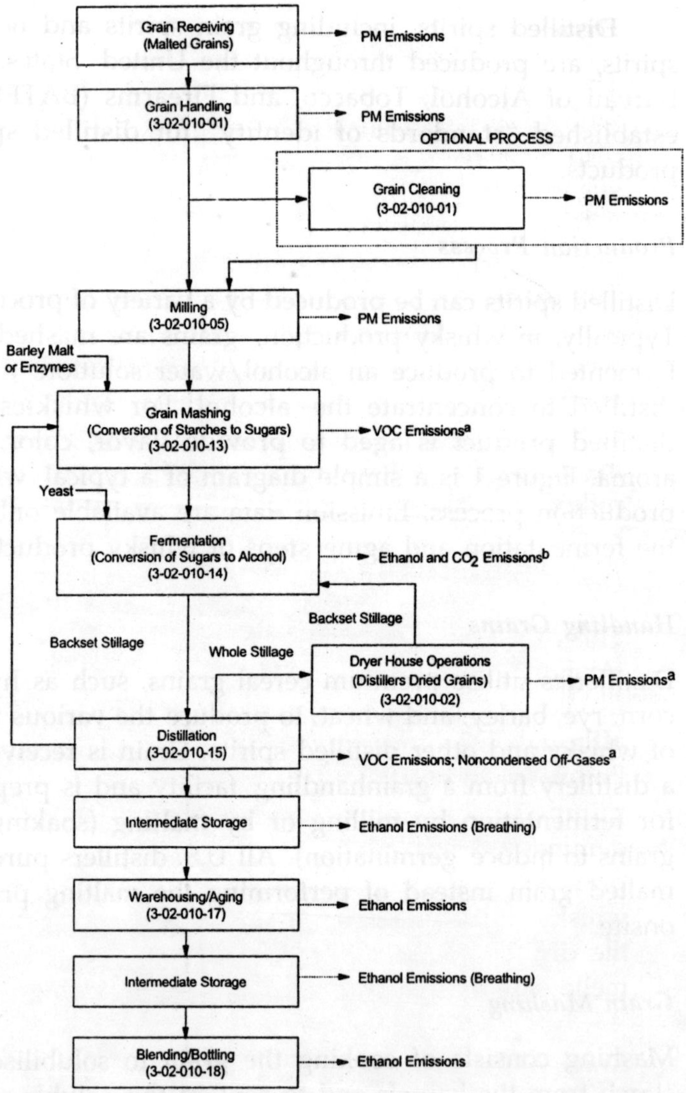

[a] Processes require heat. Emissions generated (e.g., CO, CO_2, NO_x, SO_2, PM, and VOCs) will depend on the source of fuel.
[b] Other compounds can be generated in trace quantities during fermentation including ethyl acetate, fusel oil, furfural, acetaldehyde, sulfur dioxide, and hydrogen sulfide. Acetaldehyde is a hazardous air pollutant (HAP).

Figure 1: Whisky production process

Fermentation

The converted mash enters the fermenter and is inoculated with yeast. The fermentation process, which usually lasts 3 to 5 days for whisky, uses yeast to convert the grain sugars into ethanol and carbon dioxide. Congeners are flavor compounds which are produced during fermentation as well as during the barrel aging process. The final fermented grain alcohol mixture, called "beer", is transferred to a "beer well" for holding. From the beer well, the beer passes through a preheater, where it is warmed by the alcohol vapors leaving the still, and then to the distillation unit. The beer still vapors condensed in the preheater generally are returned to the beer still as reflux.

Distillation

The distillation process separates and concentrates the alcohol from the fermented grain mash. Whisky stills are usually made of copper, especially in the rectifying section, although stainless steel may be used in some stills. Following distillation, the distilled alcohol spirits are pumped to stainless steel tanks and diluted with demineralised water to the desired alcohol concentration prior to filling into oak barrels and aging. Tennessee whisky utilises a different process from Bourbon in that the distillate is passed through sugar maple charcoal in mellowing vats prior to dilution with demineralised water.

Grain And Liquid Stillage

In most distilleries, after the removal of alcohol, still bottoms (called whole stillage), are pumped from the distillation column to a dryer house. Whole stillage may be sold, land applied (with permitting), sold as liquid feed, or processed and dried to produce distillers dried grains

(DDG) and other secondary products. Solids in the whole stillage are separated using centrifuges or screens; the liquid portion (thin stillage) may be used as a backset or concentrated by vacuum evaporation. The concentrated liquid may be recombined with the solids or dried. Drying is typically accomplished using either steam-heated or flash dryers.

Warehousing/Aging

Aging practices differ from distiller to distiller, and even for the same distiller. Variations in the aging process are integral to producing the characteristic taste of a particular brand of distilled spirit. The aging process, which typically ranges from 4 to 8 years or more, consists of storing the new whisky distillate in oak barrels to encourage chemical reactions and extractions between the whisky and the wood. The constituents of the barrel produce the whisky's characteristic color and distinctive flavor and aroma. White oak is used because it is one of the few woods that holds liquids while allowing breathing (gas exchange) through the wood. Federal law requires all Bourbon whisky to be aged in charred new white oak barrels.

The oak barrels and the barrel environment are key to producing distilled spirits of desired quality. The new whisky distillate undergoes many types of physical and chemical changes during the aging process that removes the harshness of the new distillate. As whisky ages, it extracts and reacts with constituents in the wood of the barrel, producing certain trace substances, called congeners, which give whisky its distinctive color, taste, and aroma.

Barrel environment is extremely critical in whisky aging and varies considerably by distillery, warehouse, and even location in the warehouse. Ambient atmospheric conditions, such as seasonal and diurnal variations in temperature and humidity, have a great affect on the aging process, causing changes in the equilibrium rate of extraction, rate of transfer by diffusion, and rate of reaction. As a result, distillers may expose the barrels to atmospheric conditions during certain months, promoting maturation through the selective opening of windows and doors and by other means.

Distillers often utilise various warehouse designs, including single- or multistory buildings constructed of metal, wood, brick, or masonry. Warehouses generally rely upon natural ambient temperature and humidity changes to drive the aging process. In a few warehouses, temperature is adjusted during the winter. However, whisky warehouses do not have the capability to control humidity, which varies with natural climate conditions.

Blending/Bottling

Once the whisky has completed its desired aging period, it is transferred from the barrels into tanks and reduced in proof to the desired final alcohol concentration by adding demineralised water. Following a filtration process that renders it free of any solids, the whisky is pumped to a tank in the bottling house, bottled, and readied for shipment to the distributors.

Emissions

The principal emissions from whisky production are volatile organic compounds (VOCs), principally ethanol, and occur primarily during the aging/warehousing stage. In addition to ethanol, other volatile compounds, including acetaldehyde (a HAP), ethyl acetate, glycerol, fusel oil, and furfural, may be produced in trace amounts during aging. A comparatively small source of ethanol emissions may result from the fermentation stage. Smaller quantities of ethyl acetate, isobutyl alcohol, and isoamyl alcohol are generated as well; carbon dioxide is also produced during fermentation.

Grain Elevators and Processes

Other emissions, including SO , CO , CO, NO , and PM may be generated by fuel combustion from power production facilities located at most distilled spirits plant. Ethanol and water vapor emissions result from the breathing phenomenon of the oak barrels during the aging process. This phenomenon of wood acting as a semipermeable membrane is complex and not well understood. The emissions from evaporation from the barrel during aging are not constant. During the first 6 to 18 months, the evaporation rate from a new barrel is low because the wood must become saturated (known as "soakage") before evaporation occurs.

After saturation, the evaporation rate is greatest, but then decreases as evaporation lowers the liquid level in the barrel. The lower liquid level decreases the surface area of the liquid in contact with the wood and thus reduces the surface area subject to evaporation. The rate of extraction of wood constituents, transfer, and reaction depend upon ambient conditions, such as temperature and humidity, and the concentrations of the various whisky constituents. Higher temperatures increase the rate of extraction, transfer by diffusion, and reaction.

Diurnal and seasonal temperature changes cause convection currents in the liquid. The rate of diffusion will depend upon the differences in concentrations of constituents in the wood, liquid, and air blanketing the barrel. The rates of reaction will increase or decrease with the concentration of constituents. The equilibrium concentrations of the various whisky components depend upon the humidity and air flow around the barrel. Minor emissions are generated when the whisky is drained from the barrels for blending and bottling. Residual whisky remains in the used barrels both as a surface film ("heel") and within the wood ("soakage").

For economic reasons, many distillers attempt to recover as much residual whisky as possible by methods such as rinsing the barrel with water and vacuuming. Generally, barrels are refilled and reentered into the aging process for other distilled spirits at the particular distiller or sealed with a closure (bung) and shipped offsite for reuse with other distilled spirits.

Emission Controls

With the exception of devices for controlling PM emissions, there are very few emission controls at distilleries. Grain handling and processing emissions are controlled through the use of cyclones, baghouses, and other PM control devices. There are currently no current control technologies for VOC emissions from fermenters because the significant amount of grain solids that would be carried out of the fermenters by air entrainment could quickly render systems, such as carbon adsorption, inoperable. Add-on air pollution control devices for whisky aging warehouses are not used because of potential adverse impact on product quality. Distillers ensure that barrel construction is of high quality to minimise leakage, thus reducing ethanol emissions.

Ethanol recovery would require the use of a collection system to capture gaseous emissions in the warehouse and to process the gases through a recovery system prior to venting them to the atmosphere. Because ethanol is the principal VOC emission from aging, the ethanol emissions factors are reasonable estimates of VOC emissions for these processes.

Grain Elevators and Processes

Emission factors are unavailable for grain mashing, distillation, blending/bottling, and spent grain drying. An emission factor for carbon dioxide from fermentation vats is also unavailable, although carbon dioxide and ethanol are theoretically generated in equal molecular quantities during the fermentation process.

Table 1. Emission factors for distilled spirits
Mission factor rating: E

Source	Ethanol	Ethyl acetate	Isoamyl Alcohol	Isobutyl Alcohol
Grain mashing (SCC 3-02-010-13)	NA	NA	NA	NA
Fermentation vats (SCC 3-02-010-14)	14.2	0.046	0.013	0.004
Distillation (SCC 3-02-010-15)	ND	ND	ND	ND
Aging (SCC 3-02-010-17)				
· Evaporation loss	6.9	ND	ND	ND
Blending/bottling (SCC 3-02-010-18)	ND	ND	ND	ND
Dryer house operations (SCC 3-02-010-02)	ND	ND	ND	ND

An ethanol emission factor for aging (total loss emission factor) can be calculated based on annual emissions per barrel in proof gallons (PG). The term "proof gallon" refers to a U.S. gallon of proof spirits, or the alcoholic equivalent thereof, containing 50 percent of ethyl alcohol (ethanol) by volume. This calculation method is derived from the gauging of product and measures the difference in the amount of product when the barrel was filled and when the barrel was emptied. Fugitive evaporative emissions, however, are not the sole difference between these two amounts.

During the aging period, product soaks into the barrel, test samples are drawn, and other losses (e. g., spillage, leakage) may occur. Estimates of ethanol loss due to evaporation during aging based only on the gauging of product will produce an overestimate unless soakage and sampling losses (very small losses) are subtracted.

BEER

Beer is a low potency alcoholic beverage made by fermenting grains and then extracting the liquid from the mash. Wine is a relatively low potency alcoholic beverage made by fermenting fruit juices (or other sugary liquid). Distilled spirits are high potency alcoholic beverages that are made by fermenting grains or fruit juices and then distilling the resulting liquid to reduce its water content and to concentrate its alcohol.

That may be technically correct, but it unintentionally perpetuates the myth that spirits are "harder" or more likely to lead to intoxication than are beer or wine. To prevent the misuse of alcohol, it's important for drinkers to know that standard drinks of beer, wine and spirits all contain equivalent amounts of alcohol — about six-tenths of one ounce.

A glass of white or red wine, a bottle of beer, and a shot of whiskey or other distilled spirits all contain equivalent amounts of alcohol and are they same to a Breathalyzer. A standard drink is:

— A 12-ounce bottle or can of regular beer

— A 5-ounce glass of wine

— A drink of one and 1/2 ounce of 80 proof distilled spirits (either straight or in a mixed drink)

Knowing about alcohol equivalence can help people drink in moderation. In the words of the American Dietetic Association, "Knowing the facts of beverage alcohol equivalence is a crucial aspect of responsible drinking." For example, people won't be fooled by the misleading term "hard liquor," which implies that drinking distilled spirits leads more quickly to intoxication than other alcohol beverages.

5

WINE

Wine is an alcoholic beverage that is made by fermenting grapes or grape juice. The word, wine, comes from the Latin vinum, which can mean either the "wine" or the "vine". Wine-like beverages can also be made from other fruits or from flowers, grains, and even honey, in which case, a qualifier has to be used; for example, "elderberry wine". The word wine and its equivalents in other languages is protected by law in many jurisdictions and therefore should always mean grape wine.

HISTORY OF WINE

The earliest known evidence of a fermented wine-like drink is from the Chinese village of Jiahu dated from 6000 to 7000 BC. The wine, found in 16 buried jars, contained millet, rice, beeswax (from honey) and either hawthorn fruit or wild grape. A 3,000 year old bronze jar has also been unearthed, still containing a similar liquid wine.

Wine is historically entwined with many cultures around the world. In Iran (Persia) for example, mei (the Persian wine) has been a central theme of their poetry for more than a thousand years, although alcohol is strictly forbidden in Islam.Ancient pottery jars discovered at Hajji Firuz Tepe in the Zagros Mountains of present-day Iran, near the city of Urmia, indicate that grape wine was produced as far back as 5,400 BC. It is believed that the name of the Shiraz grape originates from the Persian town of the same name. This discovery is particularly significant, as Hajji Firuz Tepe was not a grape-growing area, the main crops being grains and the preferred drink of the time was beer. As ancient Babylon was located on the Silk Road from China to the Mediterranean, all indications suggest that wine was probably used as a commodity for trade.

In ancient Egypt, wine played an important part in ceremonial life. Although wild grapes were never grown there, a thriving royal winemaking industry had been established in the Nile Delta. The industry was most likely the result of trade between Egypt and Canaan during the Early Bronze Age, commencing from at least the Third Dynasty (2650 – 2575 BC), the beginning of the Old Kingdom period (2650 – 2152 BC).

Winemaking scenes on tomb walls, and the offering lists that accompanied them, included wine that was definitely produced at the deltaic vineyards. By the end of the Old Kingdom, five wines, all probably produced in the Delta, constitute a canonical set of provisions, or fixed "menu," for the afterlife. Christianity included wine in its rites where it takes the place of the blood of Jesus, in the Mass of Orthodox, Catholic and Anglican Christians. The advent of wine in Europe was the work of the Greeks who spread the art of grape-growing and winemaking in Ancient Greece and Roman times.

Steep rock slope, Moselle RiverWine grapes grow almost exclusively between thirty and fifty north and between thirty and fifty degrees south of the Equator. The world's most southerly vineyards are in the South Island of New Zealand near the 45th parallel.

The 13 largest export nations(2005 dates) – Italy, France, Spain, Australia, Chile, the United States of

America, Germany, South Africa, Portugal, Moldova, Hungary, Croatia and Argentina. The vineyards of Algeria used to produce many fine wines, especially during and immediately after the era of French colonisation, but the resurgence of Islamic consciousness among the populace since the 1970s has greatly reduced this industry.

Classification of Wine

By Vinification Methods

Wines may be classified by vinification methods. These include classifications such as sparkling, still, fortified, rosé, and blush. The colour of wine is not determined by the juice of the grape, which is almost always clear, but rather by the presence or absence of the grape skin during fermentation. Grapes with coloured juice are known as teinturiers. Red wine is made from red (or black) grapes, but its red colour is bestowed by the skin being left in contact with the juice during fermentation. White wine can be made from any colour of grape as the skin is separated from the juice during fermentation. A white wine made from a very dark grape may appear pink or 'blush'. Rose wines are a compromise between reds and whites — the skin of red grapes is left in for a short time during fermentation.

Sparkling wines, such as champagne, are those with carbon dioxide, either from fermentation or added later. They vary from just a slight bubbliness to the classic Champagne. To have this effect, the wine is fermented twice, once in an open container to allow the carbon dioxide to escape into the air, and a second time in a sealed container, where the gas is caught and remains in the wine. Wines that gain their carbonation from the traditional method of bottle fermentation are called Méthode Traditionnelle wines in France. Other international denominations of sparkling wine include Sekt or Schaumwein (Germany), Cava (Spain), Spumante or Prosecco (Italy).

Fortified wines are often sweeter, always more alcoholic wines that have had their fermentation process stopped by the addition of a spirit, such as brandy. They include:

— Marsala
— Madeira
— Sherry
— Port

Brandy is a distilled wine. Grappa is a dry colourless brandy, distilled from fermented grape pomace, the pulpy residue of grapes, stems and seeds that were pressed for the winemaking process.

By Taste

Wines may be also classified by their primary impression on the drinker's palate. They are made up of chemical compounds which are similar to those in fruits, vegetables, and spices. Different grape varieties are associated with the aromas and tastes of different compounds. Wines may be described as 'dry' (meaning they are without sugar), off-dry, fruity, or sweet, for example.

The sweetness of wines can be measured in brix, at harvest, but is in actuality determined by the amount of residual sugar in the wine after fermentation. Dry wine, for example, has only a tiny amount of residual sugar. Specific flavors may also be sensed, at least by an experienced taster, due to the highly complex mix of organic molecules, such as esters, that a fully vinted wine contains.

By Vintage

Wines may be classified by the year in which the grapes are harvested. "Vintage wines" are made from grapes of a single year's harvest, and are accordingly dated. These wines often improve in flavor as they age, and wine enthusiasts will occasionally save bottles of a favourite vintage wine for future consumption.

For most types of wine, the best-quality grapes and the most care in wine-making are employed on vintage wines. They are therefore more expensive than non-vintage wines. Whilst vintage wines are generally made in a single batch so that each and every bottle will have a similar taste, climatic factors can have a dramatic impact on the character of a wine to the extent that different vintages from the same vineyard can vary dramatically in flavor and quality.

Superior vintages, from reputable producers and regions, will often fetch much higher prices than their average vintages. Some vintage wines are only made in better-than-average years. Conversely, wines such as White Zinfandel, which don't age well, are made to be drunk immediately and are not labeled with a vintage year. There are exceptions though. French Champagne is typically non-vintage, but may not be "cheap", and can sometimes profit from aging.

Grape Wine

Winegrapes on the vineWine is usually made from one or more varieties of the European species, Vitis vinifera. When one of these varieties, such as Pinot Noir, Chardonnay, or Zinfandel, for example, is used as the predominant grape (usually defined by law as a minimum of 75 or 85%) the result is a varietal, as opposed to a blended wine. Blended wines are in no way inferior to varietal wines; indeed, some of the world's most valued and expensive wines from the Bordeaux, Rioja or Tuscany regions, are a blend of several grape varieties of the same vintage.

Wine can also be made from Vitis labrusca, from other species or from the hybrid of two species. Vitis labrusca, Vitis aestivalis, Vitis rupestris, Vitis rotundifolia and Vitis riparia are native North American grapes, usually used for eating in fruit form or made into grape juice, but sometimes used for wine, eg. Concord wine. Hybrids of vinifera with other species were originally developed to combine American hardiness and resistance to phylloxera with European flavor. Although only rarely used and generally prohibited by law in traditional wine regions, hybrids are planted in substantial numbers in cool-climate viticultural areas.

The variety of the land, the local yeast cultures and the climate and conditions under which grapes are grown, (called "terroir") combined to offer a great variety among wine products, which are further increased by the fermentation process itself and by improvements attained with proper aging, sometimes for several decades or more. However, variety is not in itself a sought-after quality for large producers of table wine or more affordable wines, where consistency is more important for large and modern factory wines, and mass-market wine brands. Their producers will try to hide any hint of often-unremarkable "terroirs", or climatically under-performing harvest years, by:

— blending harvests of various years and vineyards;

— pasteurising the grape juice in order to kill indigenous yeasts (to be replaced with "choice" cultivated yeasts); and

— using flavor additives.

Apple Wine

Apple wine is rather unremarkable. Better to turn it into cider. Use windfall apples or, as a second choice, good quality ones. Basic recipe: 4 lbs apples, 1 lb sugar, yeast to 1 gallon water. You don't need an apple press. Cut the apples into slices, discarding grubs and cores, place in bags in the freezer. Since water expands as it freezes this will pulverise the fruit very effectively. Remove when frozen solid; place in fermentation bin. Add about a gallon of cold tap water for each 4lb of fruit. Add a few spoons of sugar and some yeast. As more apples become available, freeze them.

Don't use a food processor; we are not making apple sauce. When frozen solid, add the sliced apples in batches to the mixture. Add the rest of the sugar. Stir each day. Keep a label on the top of the bin to keep track of how much fruit/sugar have been added. When appropriate (a few days after the last addition) scoop out the apple debris with a cooking sieve—and put on the compost heap. Pour the raw cider into demijohns and continue the fermentation. When it has almost stopped, siphon or pour the cider off the sediment, into clean jars, and top up. Store in demijohns; do not bottle until a month before required. At that point, pour into screw-top plastic bottles containing 1 heaped tablespoonful of sugar for each litre.

Leave a two-inch gap at the top of each bottle. This will make it easier when opening and will avoid fountains of froth. Unscrew cautiously and slowly. It may take a few minutes for a bottle to de-gas sufficiently to pour it into a glass. As with sparkling wines, one can tell when the cider is ready to drink by the hardness of the bottle. Store them vertically, standing on a flat surface. Any bottles which fall over in store are on the point of exploding (the bottoms have bulged out); approach them with caution, slacken the tops and use promptly. If, on the other hand, you like non- gassy cider then don't add any sugar when bottling.

Two points:the cider should clear fairly quickly, but will not reach the full brightness of commercial cider (do not be put off by this; commercial ciders are clear only because they have been chemically adulterated and filtered); secondly, ciders are much better if made with acidic apples. Brews without acid are rather bland.

a) Crab apples, sliced & frozen as before. The amount can be anything from a handful to a couple of pounds per gallon depending on the must's acidity.

b) Quinces of the "japonica" type; half a dozen per gallon; the seeds removed and the quinces frozen with the apples;

c) Some under-ripe apples. These can be used as early as mid-July and need only be an inch and a half in diameter.

d) Malic acid or citric acid (less good) bought from a chemist

e) lemon juice.

In the absence of proper cider-apples varieties (and very few have access to these), Bramleys or other cooking apples make a good brew. Eating apples can obviously be mixed in. Allington Pippin and James Grieve are good because of their high acidity; Laxtons are good because of their rich flavour but make poor cider used on their own. Other fruits can contribute; one of the best ciders contained 10% over-ripe peaches, and another good brew contained more plums than apples and was coloured bright red. Use what is available; there is no point in chasing ideal ingredients when improvisation might produce a better result.

COLLECTIBLE WINES

Gold lettering on collectible Sydney Opera House wineAt the highest end, rare, super-premium wines are amongst the most expensive of all foodstuffs, and outstanding vintages from the best vineyards may sell for thousands of dollars per bottle. Red wines, at least partly because of their ability to form more complex subtleties, are typically the most expensive. Such wines are often at their best, years or sometimes decades after bottling. On the other hand, they may turn into vinegar, and before opening the bottle there may be no way of knowing this.

Part of the expense associated with high-end wine comes from the number of bottles which must be discarded in order to produce a drinkable wine. Restaurants will often charge between two to five times the price of what a wine merchant may ask for an exceptional vintage. This is for a reason: diners will often return wines that have gone foul and not bear the expense. For restaurateurs, serving old vintages is a risk that is compensated through elevated prices. Some high-end wines are Veblen goods (for conspicuous consumption).

Exclusive wines come from all the best winemaking regions of the world. Secondary markets for these wines have consequently developed, as well as specialised facilities for post-purchase storage for people to "invest" in wine. The most common wines purchased for investment are Bordeaux and Port. Many wine writers have decried the trend, as it has pushed up prices to the point that few people will consider drinking such valuable commodities, and consequently they are kept in bottles undrunk where they eventually deteriorate into a substance, very much like red wine vinegar in taste (and desirability).

Also investment in fine wine has attracted a number of fraudsters who have played on fine wine's exclusive image, and their clients' ignorance of this sector of the wine market. Typically, the scams work by charging excessively high prices on the wine, while representing that it is a sound investment unaffected by economic cycles. Like any investment, proper research is essential before investing.

Some wines, produced to mark significant events in a country or region, can also become collectible because of labelling design. An example is the Mildara Rhine Riesling produced in 1973 to mark the opening of the Sydney Opera House. Instead of labels, the bottles (red, as well as white) had printing in gold on them, as seen in the illustration.

Sparkling Wines

Add to a dry wine in a plastic bottle the necessary quantity of sugar. Replace the top, shake briefly, and return to store. When the bottle feels hard to the touch it will be sparkling. When very hard it will be like champagne. A heaped teaspoon of sugar in a one-litre bottle will produce an almost-dry sparkling wine. If a sweet sparkling wine is required then the quantities should be doubled or tripled. Bear in mind that the fermentations induced in the bottle in this way will continue until all of the sugar is used up.

Sweet sparking wines will therefore burst the bottles if not drunk promptly or de-gassed. Typically, the "priming" process, as it is called, takes from a fortnight to a month, depending on the temperature. In a cold basement or cellar it would probably take about a month; a working kitchen in winter, about a fortnight; in a hot summer a week might suffice. The method will become obvious after a few batches have been made.

Glass bottles cannot be recommended for bottling sweet wines or for the production of sparkling wines or champagne, for reasons of safety. You have been warned.

Sparkling wines (or elderflower champagne-see below) are best drunk chilled; the fizz lasts longer and the taste is less sweet.

Champagne

Champagne is a sparkling wine produced by inducing the secondary fermentation of wine. It is a sparkling wine named after the Champagne region of France. Champagne only comes from Champagne France where the community has come together to identify the best places for grapes to grow, the best types of grapes — all Champagne is produced from one or a blend of three varieties of grapes: chardonnay, pinot noir, and pinot meunier — and has identified a lengthy set of requirements that cover everything from vine pruning to the time that bottles must remain on the lees before the name Champagne can be placed on the bottle.

In Europe and most other countries, the name "champagne" is legally protected to mean only sparkling wine produced in its namesake region and adhering to the standards defined for that name as an *Appellation d'Origine Contrôlée*. There are sparkling wines made all over the world, yet many use special terms to define their own sparkling wines: Spain uses *Cava*, Italy calls it spumante, and South Africa uses *Cap Classique*.

A sparkling wine made from Muscat grapes in Italy uses the DOCG *Asti*. In Germany, Sekt is a common sparkling wine. Other sparkling wines not from Champagne sometimes use the term "sparkling wine" prominently on their label. While most countries have labeling laws that protect wine producing locations such as Champagne, some – including the United States – continue to allow US wine producers to utilize the name "Champagne" on the label of products that do not come from Champagne. This often leads to consumer confusion about genuine Champagne and is seen as deceptive by some consumers and wine experts.

Champagne's sugar content varies. The sweetest level is doux (meaning sweet), proceeding in order of increasing dryness to demi-sec (half-dry), sec (dry), extra sec (extra dry), and brut (almost completely dry). Some producers also make an extra brut or a wine with no added sugar.

Grapes used for champagne are generally picked earlier, when sugar levels are lower and acid levels higher. Except for pink or rose champagnes, the juice of harvested grapes is pressed off quickly, to keep the wine white.

The first fermentation begins in the same way as any wine, converting the natural sugar in the grapes into alcohol while the resultant carbon dioxide is allowed to escape. This produces the "base wine". This wine is not very pleasurable by itself, being too acidic. At this point the blend is assembled, using wines from various vineyards, and, in the case of non-vintage champagne, various years.

The blended wine is put in bottles along with yeast and a small amount of sugar, called the *liquor de tirage*, and stored in a wine cellar horizontally, for a second fermentation. During the secondary fermentation the carbon dioxide is trapped in the bottle, keeping it dissolved in the wine.

After ageing, they undergo a process known as *riddling* (*remuage* in French), in which they are rotated a small amount each day and gradually moved to a neck-down orientation, so that the sediment ('lees') collects in their necks and can be removed. The removal process is called "disgorging" (*dégorgement* in French), and was a skilled manual process, where the cork and the lees were removed without losing large quantities of the liquid, and a *dosage* (a varying amount of additional sugar) is added. The bottle is then recorked. Until this process was invented champagne was cloudy, a style still seen occasionally today under the label *methode ancestral*. Modern disgorgement is automated by freezing a small amount of the liquid in the neck and removing this plug of ice containing the lees.

Wines from Champagne cannot legally be sold until it has aged in the bottle for at least 18 months, but the longer the better. The majority of the Champagne produced is non-vintage, a blend of wines from several years. Typically the majority of the wine is from the current year but a percentage is made of "reserve wine" from previous years. This serves to smooth out some of the vintage variations caused by the marginal growing climate in Champagne. Most champagne houses strive for a consistent "house style" from year to year, and this is the hardest task of the winemaker. Good-quality vintage champagnes are the product of a single high-quality year, and bottles from prestigious makers can be rare and expensive.

Varieties of Champagne

Champagne is a single Appellation d'Origine Contrôlée. Grapes must be the white Chardonnay, or the red Pinot Noir or Pinot Meunier. Champagnes made exclusively from Chardonnay are known as blanc de blancs, and those exclusively from the red grapes as blanc de noirs. Champagne is typically a white wine even if it is produced with red grapes, because the juice is extracted from the grapes using a gentle process that minimizes the amount of time the juice spends in contact with the skins, which is what makes red wine red.

Rose wines are also produced, either by permitting the juice to spend more time with the skins to impart a pink color to the wine, or by adding a small amount of red wine during blending. The amount of sugar (dosage) added after the second fermentation and ageing also varies, from brut zero or brut natural, where none is added, through brut, extra-dry, sec, demi-sec and doux. The most common is brut, although in the early 20th century Champagne was generally much sweeter.

Most Champagne is non-vintage, produced from a blend of years (the exact blend is only mentioned on the label by a few growers), while that produced from a single vintage is labelled with the year and Millesime.

Many Champagnes are produced from bought-in grapes by well known brands such as Veuve Clicquot or Mumm. The identifier 'RD' on the bottle can be used to identify single growers who make their own Champagne.

Origin of Champagne

Wines from the Champagne region were already known before medieval times. Churches owned vineyards, and monks produced wine for use in the sacrament of Eucharist. French kings were traditionally anointed in Reims. Champagne wine flowed as part of coronation festivities. Kings appreciated the still, light, and crisp wine, and offered it as an homage to other monarchs in Europe.

In the 17th century, flat wines of Champagne were the chosen wines for celebration in European countries. English people were the biggest consumers of champagne wines, and drank a lot of sparkling wines. The first commercial sparkling wine was produced in the Limoux area of Languedoc about 1535. They did not invent it; nobody knows who first made it, although the British make a reasonably good claim.

Somewhere in the end of the 17th century, the sparkling method was imported in the Champagne region, associated with specific procedures for production (smooth pressing, dosage...), and stronger bottles (invented in England) that could hold the added pressure. Around 1700, sparkling champagne was born. English people loved the new sparkling wine, and spread it all other the world. *Brut* champagne, the modern champagne, was created for the British in 1876. The Russian royalty also consumed huge quantities.

Bubbles

Bubbles in champagne are commonly believed to be formed in impurities in the glass that act as nucleation sites. However, these impurities are actually too small as shown by Gerard Liger-Belair, Richard Marchal, and Philippe Jeandel with a high-speed video camera. Bubbles most readily form on scratches or nicks in the glass, which are frequently made intentionally by the manufacturer or the end user to provide nucleation sites. Dom Perignon was originally charged by his wine-making Abbey of Hautvillers to get the bubbles out of their champagne.

Champagne bottles

Champagne is mostly fermented in two sizes bottles, standard bottle (750 mL), and Magnum (1.5 L). In general, magnums are thought to be higher quality, as there is less oxygen in the bottle, and the volume to surface area favors the creation of appropriately-sized bubbles. However, there is no hard evidence for this view. Other bottle sizes, named for Biblical figures, are generally filled with champagne that has been fermented in standard bottles or magnums.

The deliberate spraying of champagne has become an integral part of sports trophy presentations and locker room celebrations, though champagne enthusiasts sometimes cringe at the waste. To reduce the risk of spilling champagne and/or turning the cork into a projectile, open a champagne bottle as follows:

— Remove the foil;

— Place your hand over the cork;
— Loosen but don't remove the wire cage;
— Grasp the cork and the cage firmly with your hand, then rotate the bottle (rather than the cork) by holding it at the base; this should allow the cork to come out on its own accord.

The desired effect is to ease the cork out with a satisfying *pop* rather than to shoot the cork across the room or produce a fountain of foamy wine. Some wine connoisseurs prefer that the ideal way to open a bottle of champagne is to do it so carefully and gently that no sound is emitted at all. A legendary method, used with great ceremony when opening a champagne bottle, is the use of a sabre. To properly execute, one should:

i) Select a heavy sabre, with a rather short blade and broad back;

ii) Hold in one hand the sabre. Use the back and not the cut of the blade;

iii) Hold in the other hand the champagne bottle on its lowest part, the wire cage loosened;

iv) Touch and slide the blade alongside the bottle until it hits the swelling on the bottleneck. The jolt will break the bottle and its tip will fly away in a trajectory;

v) Have part of the spray spill out in order to wash away potential glass splinters;

vi) Using the sabre method is not particular difficult, but some precautions are necessary:

vii) The sabre is a weapon and might be dangerous;

viii) The tip of the bottle will fly away with force. Keep the forseen trajectory free of obstacles;

ix) Check fluid for glass splinters before drinking;

Serving Champagne

Champagne is usually served in a champagne flute, whose characteristics include a long stem with a tall, narrow bowl and opening. The wider flat glass (cup) commonly associated with champagne is no longer preferred by connoisseurs because it does not preserve the bubbles and aroma of the wine as well. But champagne is better for tasting with a big red wine glass (i.e. a glass for bordeaux), as the aroma spreads better in the large area of the glass, but contrary to the cup, the aroma stays in the glass.

Champagne is always served cold, and is best at the temperature 7C° (43 to 48°F). Often the bottle is chilled in a bucket of ice and water before and after opening. Champagne buckets are made specifically for this purpose.

Quick Cooling of Sparkling Wines

Sparkling wine is a wine with significant levels of carbon dioxide in it making it fizzy. The carbon dioxide results from natural fermentation, either in a bottle as with the methode champenoise, or in a large tank designed to withstand the pressures involved, as in the charmat process. In some parts of the world, the word champagne is used as a synonym for sparkling wine, although some prefer to reserve the word champagne for a specific type from the Champagne region of France.

The classic example of a sparkling wine is Champagne, but many other examples are produced in other countries and regions, such as sekt in Germany, cava in Spain, spumante in Italy, Cap Classique in South Africa. Sparkling wine is usually white or rose but there are several examples of red Australian sparkling shiraz.

Unfortunately, because of economic realities, the sparkling wines at weddings is by necessity drunk more out of custom than for the taste. This is not necessary.

All wines which undergo a second fermentation (and are thus carbonated) are sparkling wines. Only sparkling wines made in Champagne, France, are properly called champagnes. All "champagnes" are rather expensive and one can seldom go wrong with any true champagne.

You can cool down any white wine quickly by filling a sink with enough ice and water to cover the bottle. Don't use ice alone. The presence of the water is necessary for quick cooling. Lay the bottle in the iced water and twirl it for two to four minutes or let it stand for about ten minutes.

Glassware

Sparkling wines are drunk as much for their apperances as their taste. Great appearance cannot overcome lousy taste, but why miss those heavenly stars? The proper glass can emphasize the bubbles of any sparkling wine. The goal is a clear, totally dry glass, with tall sides which come to a point on the inside at the bottom.

White wine glasses will do in a pinch, but a champagne glass is worth the investment. There are two Baccarat champagne glasses (expensive) for those romantic special occasions. One should also have a set of six less expensive champagne glasses for small dinners, etc. Wipe the glasses with a dry, lint-free cloth before serving and make sure the glasses are totally dry. Water ruins the visual effect of sparkling wines. And don't chill the glasses. They will fog up and cloud the view.

But what about the typical champagne glasses you see in the movies? You know the ones. They are about three inches across the opening and about 2 inches deep. They are called Cleopatra glasses. They are too shallow and too wide to concentrate the bubbles to best effect. And they allow the champagne to cool off too quickly. The only good thing about them is the story behind their name. It is said that their form is based on the shape of Cleopatra's breasts.

Removing the cork

Don't forget the laws of physics when removing a cork from a bottle of sparkling wine. Get a cloth towel and drap it over the neck of the bottle while you carefully remove the foil and the metal wine cage. Be aware that on rare occasions the cork will shoot out like a bullet. The cloth helps prevent injury . Watch where you "point" the bottle.

The key to elegant cork removal is to pat the bottle dry, grasp the cork with the towel (the same one you will circle the bottle with for pouring) and twist the bottle, not the cork. One can usually feel the cork coming free. With practice one can ease the cork out at the last second to time a perfectly controlled "pop"-to the delight of all watching.

Gentle twisting of the bottle will usually prevent fizz going everywhere. Although Hollywood likes the fizz to geyser out of the bottle one loses much carbonation with this trick, not to mention the mess on clothing, furniture and flooring. The show is in the glass, not in the foam.

Resealing

There is no rule that says a bottle of sparkling wine must be drunk once opened. Most sparkling wines will still have fizz for approximately twelve hours. So the bottle you open tonight will still be good tomorrow morning if you reseal it properly. And the only way to do that is with a special champagne cork made of metal with a spring and special lip to grab the rim of the bottle. These champagne corks are available at fine wine stores everywhere. Champagne sealers cost about $7.00 and are well worth it. Remember, you are drinking a sparkling wine for the romance, not to get drunk. A champagne cork allows that romance to be experienced both at night and in the morning!

Winemaking

For winemaking, you will need is plenty of space. You will also need a source of fruit, a few demijohns picked up for very little at a car boot sale, some airlocks or pierced bungs, a siphon, and a couple of 2-gallon or 5-gallon containers with lids. Any winemaking shop, and many chemists, can supply the basic implements. If you wish to put finished wine in glass bottles you will need a good corking tool.

You will also need a modicum of patience and the odd hour or two of spare time. But remember that this is not an activity which needs lots of time. Once one is organised, the time required is quite minimal; in perhaps an hour or so once a month make around 20 gallons a year plus 10 gallons of cider.

Fruit Wines

Ingredients: 3-4 lbs fruit, 2 lbs sugar, 8 oz raisins, currants or sultanas, and yeast makes one gallon.

Procedure

Prepare the fruit

The fruit must be free from spoilage organisms. Failure to remove them may result in the wine turning to vinegar. There are three ways of killing them: a) Boiling b) Freezing c) Chemical sterilisation. Spotlessly clean fruit can be sterilised by pouring boiling water over it, but fruit of winemaking grade will not be bacteria-free after doing this;

boiling or freesing will be necessary. Do not use your best fruit for winemaking; the product is no better.

Boiling

Works well with dark red fruit, especially elderberries and mulberries. The juice is strained off and the pulp discarded .Not to be recommended in fruits of delicate flavour. Wines produced from boiled fruit can suffer from two drawbacks: a) very slow to clear; often a year or two: this is why you need storage space; b) less bouquet; but for making full-bodied reds it works well. Wines made in this way are often sweet and do not ferment out fully.

Freezing

Two days in the freezer will result in most fresh fruit being reduced to the ideal state for fermentation. Wines produced in this way tend to have a stronger bouquet and clear rapidly. Cherry wines, for example, frequently clear in a month.

Chemical sterilisation

Not recommended. A principal attraction of home-made wines is that the sulphurous after-taste of cheaper commercial wines (especially whites) is absent. If you prefer chemically sterilised wine, buy commercial.

Starting the fermentation

Place the 3lbs (or more) of prepared fruit in a fermentation bin; usually straight from the freezer but occasionally boiled (or in the case of peelable fruit, fresh-for example, banana or pineapple). Add a few pints of cold water. Meanwhile simmer 8 oz of sultanas (or, less good, raisins or currants) for 30 minutes in about a pint of water. Then pour into the fruit mixture. Add cold water until the total volume is just over a gallon. Add nutrient and stir. Add tannin if the fruit doesn't contain any. (don't buy it-a few fruit stalks, stones or cores will do the job). Sprinkle in some yeast, or add a cupful of mixture from another brew, stir again, and then cover. After a couple of days the fermentation should have started. Stir vigorously once a day for about 4 days.

Some fruits contain pectin (e.g. bananas, redcurrants, apples, sloes, cherries) and this will make the wine cloudy, especially if they have been boiled. A pectin-destroying enzyme can be added with such fruit, or the wine may be reluctant to clear. It is added at the same time as the yeast (but see note at end) Do not forget to label the jar. A snap-around label which fits around the demi-john handle can be made as follows from a piece of plastic from a detergent bottle or similar; this can easily be transferred from jar to jar during racking, and sticky labels will adhere to it. Write in pencil, so that spillages don't render it unreadable.

Dried Grape

Failure to use some form of grape in the mixture may result in an anaemic wine. The following factors are helpful:

Raisins are dried red grapes. Their flavour is quite strong and results in the finished wine having a strong hint of sherry in its makeup. It is most noticeable when the other ingredients have weak flavours. If you dislike sherry, raisins should be avoided. Currants are smaller dried red grapes with a very strong flavour. They are not generally recommended, but tolerable in elderberry brews.

Sultanas are dried white grapes. Their flavour is relatively weak (though not negligible) and is not carried over too much into the product wine. But again, unless one is aiming at something with the character of a sherry or port, 8 oz per gallon is enough.

Those lucky enough to have fresh grapes available can use 1-2 lb per gallon instead of 8 oz. dried fruit. Grape concentrates can be used to produce excellent wines, but they are five or six times the price of dried grapes. One should not encourage extortion. Pineapple juice is a good grape substitute; gooseberry less good.

After 4 Days

Scoop out the fruit debris with a cooking sieve. Put on the compost heap; it is an excellent activator. Sterilise a demi-john with a weak solution of non-scented disinfectant and rinse out three times with a pint of water A disinfectant smelling of chlorine is the most suitable. Do not waste money on Campden tablets. Using a funnel, pour the fermenting mixture into the demi-john, which should become about three quarters full, and immediately seal with a fermentation lock. For the first day or two, foaming may occur. When the fermentation starts to slow down, top up to one gallon. If any foam or other debris reaches the bung, remove it with a small teaspoon.

A good fermentation lock may be made as follows: Obtain a rubber bung with a hole in it; stick two layers of waterproof insulation tape over the hole, and make two small perforations with a pin or knife point in the tape. This bung will let gas out but will not let flies in.

After a week or so, debris will be largely settled. When the fermentation stops (or nearly stops) and the wine starts to clear, siphon or pour off the top layer into a second clean jar. Top up again with cold water. This process ("racking") is carried out as many times as is necessary, typically about three, until the wine is ready for bottling. To rack a substantial quantity in jars using a siphon you will need two empties. This means you can wash one whilst the other is siphoning. If you are concerned that racking dilutes the wine too much, top up with apple or pineapple juice rather than water. Pineapple top-ups give the wine an excellent bouquet; a litre costs about £1 and contains enough for about 6 demijohns.

Bottling

Taste a little of the wine. It may taste very unpleasant at this stage, but you should be able to tell whether or not any sugar is left. If sweet, it is not ready to bottle. If completely dry to the taste, hold it to the light. Is it still producing any gas? If so, it is still not ready to bottle if you want a still wine. One must be patient; sometimes a wait of a year or so is necessary.

a)*Glass*: However, if you must use glass, get a decent corker-the sort with a long lever- otherwise corking becomes a tiresome, difficult chore. Warm the corks in water on the stove for a minute or two to soften them. Leave the bottled wine upright for a day or two for the corks to harden, then cover with clingfilm and tape round, or rub the top of the corks with vaseline and drip candlewax until it seals. Lay the bottles down if you wish, but if they are properly sealed this is not necessary. Mine are nearly all stored upright, and the corks never dry out: if properly sealed, they can't. Note that sweet wines should only be bottled in plastic. Refermentation may cause explosions and flying glass unless chemicals are used to kill the yeast.

b)*Plastic (Screw-top)*: These bottles are also useful for ciders. A demijohn will fill completely two two-litre bottles, or four one-litre bottles. The most suitable are those used for lemonade and tonic water. The smaller ones (half-litre) can be used for beers; more on this later. Obviously one does not serve wine from plastic containers at the table any more than one keeps a dustbin in the kitchen. But a two-litre bottle will fill three decanters (or one decanter three times) and this can be done the day before use. There are advantages to using plastic bottles:

a) Ease of sealing;

b) No danger if gases build up and the bottle bursts (glass bottles can explode like grenades);

c) Sparkling wines can be made easily, or even fair imitations of champagne.

They are also rather larger than standard 750 ml wine bottles; a gallon of wine consequently takes up less space in storage. They will store upright or flat, but should be allowed to stand upright for a week or two before use, to allow sediment to settle. If used more than once, the tops and the screw threads of the bottles must be sterilised in disinfectant; this is where bacteria hide. Pour some disinfectant in a bowl, pour some more in each bottle and loosely screw on the top. Invert the bottles in the bowl and leave for a few minutes.

Cowslip Wine

Ingredients—To every gallon of water allow 3 lbs. of lump sugar, the rind of 2 lemons, the juice of 1, the rind and juice of 1 Seville orange, 1 gallon of cowslip pips. To every 4-1/2 gallons of wine allow 1 bottle of brandy.

Mode—Boil the sugar and water together for 1/2 hour, carefully removing all the scum as it rises. Pour this boiling liquor on the orange and lemon-rinds, and the juice, which should be strained; when milk-warm, add the cowslip pips or flowers, picked from the stalks and seeds; and to 9 gallons of wine 3 tablespoonfuls of good fresh brewers' yeast. Let it ferment 3 or 4 days; then put all together in a cask with the brandy, and let it remain for 2 months, when bottle it off for use.

Elder Wine

Ingredients—To every 3 gallons of water allow 1 peck of elderberries; to every gallon of juice allow 3 lbs. of sugar, 1/2 oz. of ground ginger, 6 cloves, 1 lb. of good Turkey raisins; 1/2 pint of brandy to every gallon of wine. To every 9 gallons of wine 3 or 4 tablespoonfuls of fresh brewer's yeast.

Mode—Pour the water, quite boiling, on the elderberries, which should be picked from the stalks, and let these stand covered for 24 hours; then strain the whole through a sieve or bag, breaking the fruit to express all the juice from it. Measure the liquor, and to every gallon allow the above proportion of sugar. Boil the juice and sugar with the ginger, cloves, and raisins for 1 hour, skimming the liquor the whole time; let it stand until milk-warm, then put it into a clean dry cask, with 3 or 4 tablespoonfuls of good fresh yeast to every 9 gallons of wine. Let it ferment for about a fortnight; then add the brandy, bung up the cask, and let it stand some months before it is bottled, when it will be found excellent. A bunch of hops suspended to a string from the bung, some persons say, will preserve the wine good for several years. Elder wine is usually mulled, and served with sippets of toasted bread and a little grated nutmeg.

Elderberry Wine

The elderberry is well adapted for the production of wine; its juice contains a considerable portion of the principle necessary for a vigorous fermentation, and its beautiful colour communicates a rich tint to the wine made from it. It is, however, deficient in sweetness, and therefore demands an addition of sugar. It is one of the very best of the genuine old English wines; and a cup of it mulled, just previous to retiring to bed on a winter night, is a thing to be "run for," It is not, however, agreeable to every taste.

Effervescing Gooseberry Wine

Ingredients—To every gallon of water allow 6 lbs. of green gooseberries, 3 lbs. of lump sugar.

Mode—This wine should be prepared from unripe gooseberries, in order to avoid the flavour which the fruit would give to the wine when in a mature state. Its briskness depends more upon the time of bottling than upon the unripe state of the fruit, for effervescing wine can be made from fruit that is ripe as well as that which is unripe. The fruit should be selected when it has nearly attained its full growth, and consequently before it shows any tendency to ripen.

Any bruised or decayed berries, and those that are very small, should be rejected. The blossom and stalk ends should be removed, and the fruit well bruised in a tub or pan, in such quantities as to insure each berry being broken without crushing the seeds. Pour the water (which should be warm) on the fruit, squeeze and stir it with the hand until all the pulp is removed from the skin and seeds, and cover the whole closely for 24 hours; after which, strain it through a coarse bag, and press it with as much force as can be conveniently applied, to extract the whole of the juice and liquor the fruit may contain.

To every 40 or 50 lbs. of fruit one gallon more of hot water may be passed through the marc, or husks, in order to obtain any soluble matter that may remain, and be again pressed. The juice should be put into a tub or pan of sufficient size to contain all of it, and the sugar added to it. Let it be well stirred until the sugar is dissolved, and place the pan in a warm situation; keep it closely covered, and let it ferment for a day or two. It must then be drawn off into clean casks, placed a little on one side for the scum that arises to be thrown out, and the casks kept filled with the remaining "must," that should be reserved for that purpose.

When the active fermentation has ceased, the casks should be plugged upright, again filled, if necessary, the bungs be put in loosely, and, after a few days, when the fermentation is a little more languid, the bungs should be driven in tight, and a spile-hole made, to give vent if necessary. About November or December, on a clear fine day, the wine should he racked from its lees into clean casks, which may be rinsed with brandy. After a month, it should be examined to see if it is sufficiently clear for bottling; if not, it must be fined with isinglass, which may be dissolved in some of the wine: 1 oz. will be sufficient for 9 gallons. In March or April, or when the gooseberry bushes begin to blossom, the wine must be bottled, in order to insure its being effervescing.

Blackberry

Bright red wine a little more fruity and less port-like than elderberry. Add lemon juice/ malic acid/tartaric acid for acidity, or some crab apples. That a mixture of 2lb blackberries plus a pineapple (or 1 litre pineapple juice) makes a good brew even without sultanas or raisins.

Loganberry

Similar to blackberry wine but lighter in colour. The flavour is excellent and the bouquet is a little stronger.

Strawberry

A good wine which takes about three years to reach its best; very young strawberry wines are bland and somewhat disappointing. Remember to add enough acid. The wine is better if blackberries are added.

Mlberry

Mulberries are harvested by gathering up windfalls or by shaking the tree. They will not drop off until overripe, and most mulberry trees are too large for easy access. The fruit must be sterilised thoroughly by freezing or boiling because much of it will have been walked on by fruit flies. A couple of bananas will improve the brew.

The wine which results is rich in flavour and bouquet; red to deep red-brown, and often resembles sherry. It can take a long time to clear, and leave it for at least 3 years before drinking. The flavour of mulberries is strong, and this wine is one where raisins can be used without spoiling the flavour. Tannin additions are unnecessary. But not everyone will like this one; mulberries are an acquired taste.

Ginger Wine

Ingredients—To 9 gallons of water allow 27 lbs. of loaf sugar, 9 lemons, 12 oz. of bruised ginger, 3 tablespoonfuls of yeast, 2 lbs. of raisins stoned and chopped, 1 pint of brandy.

Mode—Boil together for 1 hour in a copper (let it previously be well scoured and beautifully clean) the water, sugar, lemon-rinds, and bruised ginger; remove every particle of scum as it rises, and when the liquor is sufficiently boiled, put it into a large tub or pan, as it must not remain in the copper. When nearly cold, add the yeast, which must be thick and very fresh, and, the next day, put all in a dry cask with the strained lemon-juice and chopped raisins. Stir the wine every day for a fortnight; then add the brandy, stop the cask down by degrees, and in a few weeks it will be fit to bottle.

Lemon Wine

Ingredients—To 4-1/2 gallons of water allow the pulp of 50 lemons, the rind of 25, 16 lbs. of loaf sugar,— 1/2 oz. of isinglass, 1 bottle of brandy.

Mode—Peel and slice the lemons, but use only the rind of 25 of them, and put them into the cold water. Let it stand 8 or 9 days, squeezing the lemons well every day; then strain the water off and put it into a cask with the sugar. Let it work some time, and when it has ceased working, put in the isinglass. Stop the cask down; in about six months put in the brandy and bottle the wine off.

Malt Wine

Ingredients—5 gallons of water, 28 lbs. of sugar, 6 quarts of sweet-wort, 6 quarts of tun, 3 lbs. of raisins, 1/2 lb. of candy, 1 pint of brandy.

Mode—Boil the sugar and water together for 10 minutes; skim it well, and put the liquor into a convenient-sized pan or tub. Allow it to cool; then mix it with the sweet-wort and tun. Let it stand for 3 days, then put it into a barrel; here it will work or ferment for another three days or more; then bung up the cask, and keep it undisturbed for 2 or 3 months.

After this, add the raisins (whole), the candy, and brandy, and, in 6 months' time, bottle the wine off. Those who do not brew, may procure the sweet-wort and tun from any brewer. Sweet-wort is the liquor that leaves the mash of malt before it is boiled with the hops; tun is the new beer after the whole of the brewing operation has been completed.

Superior Orange Wine

Ingredients—90 Seville oranges, 32 lbs. of lump sugar, water.

Mode—Break up the sugar into small pieces, and put it into a dry, sweet 9-gallon cask, placed in a cellar or other storehouse, where it is intended to be kept. Have ready close to the cask two large pans or wooden keelers, into one of which put the peel of the oranges pared quite thin, and into the other the pulp after the juice has been squeezed from it. Strain the juice through a piece of double muslin, and put it into the cask with the sugar. Then pour about 1-1/2 gallon of cold spring water on both the peels and pulp; let it stand for 24 hours, and then strain it into the cask; add more water to the peels and pulp when this is done, and repeat the same process every day for a week: it should take about a week to fill up the cask. Be careful to apportion the quantity as nearly as possible to the seven days, and to stir the contents of the cask each day. On the "third' day after the cask is full,— that is, the 'tenth' day after the commencement of making,— the cask may be securely bunged down. This is a very simple and easy method, and the wine made according to it will be pronounced to be most excellent.

There is no troublesome boiling, and all fermentation takes place in the cask. When the above directions are attended to, the wine cannot fail to be good. It should be bottled in 8 or 9 months, and will be fit for use in a twelve month after the time of making. Ginger wine may be made in precisely the same manner, only, with the 9-gallon cask for ginger wine, 2 lbs. of the best whole ginger, 'bruised', must be put with the sugar.

Rhubarb Wine

Ingredients—To every 5 lbs. of rhubarb pulp allow 1 gallon of cold spring water; to every gallon of liquor allow 3 lbs. of loaf sugar, 1/2 oz. of isinglass, the rind of 1 lemon.

Mode—Gather the rhubarb about the middle of May; wipe it with a wet cloth, and, with a mallet, bruise it in a large wooden tub or other convenient means. When reduced to a pulp, weigh it, and to every 5 lbs. add 1 gallon of cold spring water; let these remain for 3 days, stirring 3 or 4 times a day; and, on the fourth day, press the pulp through a hair sieve; put the liquor into a tub, and to every gallon put 3 lbs. of loaf sugar; stir in the sugar until it is quite dissolved, and add the lemon-rind; let the liquor remain, and, in 4, 5, or 6 days, the fermentation will begin to subside, and a crust or head will be formed, which should be skimmed off, or the liquor drawn from it, when the crust begins to crack or separate.

Put the wine into a cask, and if, after that, it ferments, rack it off into another cask, and in a fortnight stop it down. If the wine should have lost any of its original sweetness, add a little more loaf sugar, taking care that the cask is full. Bottle it off in February or March, and in the summer it should be fit to drink. It will improve greatly by keeping; and, should a very brilliant colour be desired, add a little currant-juice.

Clarets

All those wines called in England clarets are the produce of the country round Bordeaux, or the Bordelais; but it is remarkable that there is no pure wine in France known by the name of claret, which is a corruption of *clairet*, a term that is applied there to any red or rose-coloured wine. Round Bordeaux are produced a number of wines of the first quality, which pass under the name simply of *vins de Bordeaux*, or have the designation of the particular district where they are made; as Lafitte, Latour, &c. The clarets brought to the English market are frequently prepared for it by the wine-growers by mixing together several Bordeaux wines, or by adding to them a portion of some other wines; but in France the pure wines are carefully preserved distinct. The genuine wines of Bordeaux are of great variety, that part being one of the most distinguished in France; and the principal vineyards are those of Medoc, Palus, Graves, and Blanche, the product of each having characters considerably different.

Negus

Ingredients—To every pint of port wine allow 1 quart of boiling water, 1/4 lb. of sugar, 1 lemon, grated nutmeg to taste.

Mode—As this beverage is more usually drunk at children's parties than at any other, the wine need not be very old or expensive for the purpose, a new fruity wine answering very well for it. Put the wine into a jug, rub some lumps of sugar (equal to 1/4 lb.) on the lemon-rind until all the yellow part of the skin is absorbed, then squeeze the juice, and strain it. Add the sugar and lemon-juice to the port wine, with the grated nutmeg; pour over it the boiling water, cover the jug, and, when the beverage has cooled a little, it will be fit for use. Negus may also be made of sherry, or any other sweet white wine, but is more usually made of port than of any other beverage.

Mull Wine

Ingredients— To every pint of wine allow 1 large cupful of water, sugar and spice to taste.

Mode—In making preparations like the above, it is very difficult to give the exact proportions of ingredients like sugar and spice, as what quantity might suit one person would be to another quite distasteful. Boil the spice in the water until the flavour is extracted, then add the wine and sugar, and bring the whole to the boiling-point, when serve with strips of crisp dry toast, or with biscuits. The spices usually used for mulled wine are cloves, grated nutmeg, and cinnamon or mace. Any kind of wine may be mulled, but port and claret are those usually selected for the purpose; and the latter requires a very large proportion of sugar.

The vessel that the wine is boiled in must be delicately clean, and should be kept exclusively for the purpose. Small tin warmers may be purchased for a trifle, which are more suitable than saucepans, as, if the latter are not scrupulously clean, they will spoil the wine, by imparting to it a very disagreeable flavour. These warmers should be used for no other purposes.

Banana Wine

A good use for cheap, over-ripe bananas from the local fruit shop or market stall. The wine is pleasant and light with a good bouquet. Don't forget to add plenty of acid and some tannin. Best after two or three years.

Mixed Fruit

A good table wine can be made by emptying the freezer of unused fruit once a year, and mixing it together in one large brew. Mixed soft fruit is the most successful. Don't include rhubarb. Similarly, don't add too many gooseberries, as these will swamp other flavours, and don't use plums or damsons; these are best kept for adding to cider brews or treating separately. Plums are sometimes oily when fermented, and brews containing them can be difficult to clear."Plum Cider" is worth making if plums are available.

Cherry Wine

Cherries cost a fortune to buy in winemaking quantities and this is not usually a viable option. In any case, eating varieties are not the best to use; Morellos are better.

Japonica Quince Wine

Quinces must be boiled or frozen before use. Their flavour is pleasant but overpowering, and although they can make a good wine they are best used in moderation (8 ozs or so per gallon maximum) in conjunction with other fruit or as an ingredient of cider.

Drinking the Wine

a)Long-term storage

If you have adequate storage facilities-say a cellar, garage or basement capable of holding a couple of hundred bottles- try to leave all wines for at least 18 months or so before drinking. Keep dark if possible; red wines are bleached to some extent by light. Most wines, particularly the reds, will improve for several years, and the initial harsh tastes of elderberry, blackberry and mulberry especially will become much softer and mellow. Five-year-old elderberry/ blackberry/ apple wine when well-made is almost indistinguishable from good quality Australian or French reds. Other five-year-old wines (strawberry, mulberry, banana) are better in flavour than mass-exported grape wines.

b)Decanting

It is vandalism to unseal a bottle of wine and to drink it straight away. This applies to any wine. To take a commercial example, a good auslese (a high-class German white wine) is better if opened the day before use, poured off the sediment into a decanter, then placed in the 'fridge until the next day.(If the original bottle needs to be used at table, it should be rinsed out; the wine poured back into it and taken out of the fridge an hour or so before use). A really good wine of this type will improve perceptibly for several days, after opening, if properly stored, and will keep in excellent condition for about a fortnight before it starts to deteriorate.

A friend of mine with a good wine cellar used to reckon that the best German wine improved, after opening, for about the same number of days as its age in years. The same principle applies in some measure to all wines, whether commercial or home brewed. When a bottle is opened, it takes time for the volatile compounds in the wine to be released, and for the final traces of harshness to disappear. Opening a wine the day before it is needed will almost always result in a significant improvement in flavour. Proprietors of eating houses will not thank you for telling them.

A further point is that undecanted wines are unsuitable for transporting in the back of the car if they are to be drunk that day. The sediment is disturbed and the wine when opened will be below its best. If a red, it may be undrinkable. If invited to a friend's and taking wine specifically for the meal (especially home-brewed), decant it first. And make sure that the host has not already decanted enough wine from his own stocks. He may prefer to use that and save yours for another occasion.

c)The Correct Temperature

Whites are best served slightly chilled (not refrigerated), after several hours on the cellar floor, or at least a cold floor. Ice buckets are an affectation which does nothing useful for a wine. Reds are best at room temperature.

Those who regularly brew and drink their own wines find many supermarket wines harshly flavoured and sulphury. Cheap wines induce headaches in cases of over-indulgence, perhaps because of the chemicals they contain.

6

COCKTAILS

Cocktail is a stimulating liquor composed of spirits of any kind, sugar, water, and bitters—it is vulgarly called a bittered sling and is supposed to be an excellent electioneering potion, inasmuch as it renders the heart stout and bold, at the same time that it fuddles the head. It is said, also to be of great use to a Democratic candidate: because a person, having swallowed a glass of it, is ready to swallow anything else.

A cocktail is a mix of several substances, usually liquids. It usually containing one or more distilled alcoholic beverages and perhaps non-alcoholic drinks, ice and sometimes liqueur, fruit, sauce, honey, milk or cream, spices, etc. The cocktail became popular during Prohibition in the United States; to mask the taste of bootlegged alcohol, the bartenders at a speakeasy would mix it with other liquors and non-alcoholic drinks.

Until the 1970s, cocktails were made predominantly with gin, whiskey, or rum, and rarely vodka. From the 1970s on, the popularity of vodka increased dramatically. By the 1980s it was the predominant base for mixed drinks. Many cocktails traditionally made with gin, such as the gimlet, may now be served by default with vodka. Non-alcoholic carbonated beverages which are nearly exclusively used in cocktails (or in non-alcoholic soda fountain drinks, such as the egg cream) include soda water, tonic water and seltzer. Liqueurs are also common cocktail ingredients. In addition to listings of recipes for Punches, Sours, Slings, Cobblers, Shrubs, Toddies, Flips, and a variety of other types of mixed drinks were 10 recipes for drinks referred to as "Cocktails".

A cocktail

A key ingredient which differentiated "cocktails" from other drinks in this compendium, was the use of bitters as an ingredient, although it is not to be seen in very many modern cocktail recipes. During Prohibition in the United States, when alcohol consumption was illegal, cocktails were still consumed in establishments known as speakeasies. Not only was the quality of the alcohol available far lower than was previously used, but the skill and knowledge of the bartenders would also decline significantly during this time.

A partial list of cocktails are given below. As a normal matter of course, only cocktails with a particularly significant history are assigned.

Cocktails with Beer

Black and Tan

Black and Tan is a cocktail made from equal parts English bitter (ale) and Irish stout, with the stout most commonly being Guinness. The name is an allusion to the Black and Tans, soldiers sent to Ireland by the British government in the early 1920s to suppress Sinn Féin revolutionaries agitating for Irish independence.

The most common Black and Tan in the United States uses Guinness stout and Bass ale. The stout is "layered" on top of the ale, taking advantage of their differing densities. This is accomplished by first halfway filling the glass with ale, then adding the stout. The top layer is best poured slowly over an upside-down tablespoon placed over the glass to avoid splashing and mixing the layers.

Combining Guinness and Harp lager (instead of Bass) results in a "Half and half." A "black and white" is a stout with any lager or ale. A similar beverage using champagne as one of the mixers is the black velvet, which consists of half champagne and half stout. A "poor man's black velvet" subsitutes hard apple cider for the champagne. This variation is also called a "snakebite" by some.

Despite the use of what is arguably Ireland's national beer, the drink is relatively unknown in Ireland and an attempt to order it in a pub there would likely result in either teasing for adulterating the Guinness, or hostility due to the historical relevance of the name.

Black Velvet

The black velvet, also known as a Bismarck, is a cocktail made from a stout beer (often Guinness) and a white, sparkling wine, traditionally champagne. A black velvet is made by filling a tall flute glass halfway full of chilled stout and floating the sparkling wine on top of the stout, with the differing densities of the liquids allowing them to remain largely in separate layers.

Apple cider or perry is sometimes used in place of the more expensive champagne, in which case the stout is floated on top of the cider or perry. This cocktail is known as a Poor man's black velvet. Whatever the top layer is, the effect is best achieved if it is poured over a spoon turned upside down over the top of the glass so that the liquid runs gently down the sides rather than splashing into the lower layer and mixing with it.

A similar effect is achieved by mixing a dark and a light-coloured beer in the black and tan cocktail, though the more similar specific gravities allow for less distinct layers. According to Brewer's Dictionary of Phrase and Fable, the black velvet was the favourite drink of Otto von Bismarck, who supposedly drank it by the gallon. In Germany, the cocktail often goes by his name.

Boiler

Ingredients

— 1 shot of Whiskey, or any other spirit.

— 1 pint of Beer of your choice.

Procedure

— Hold the shot of spirits above pint glass of Beer, drop, and chug.

Flaming Dr. Pepper

The Flaming Dr. Pepper is a flaming cocktail that tastes like the soft drink Dr Pepper, although it does not contain any. This drink inspired an episode of the animated television show The Simpsons. The analogous drink on that episode was known at first as the "Flaming Homer," later as the "Flaming Moe" (for the programme's bartender).

Equipment

— pint glass
— shot glass
— cigarette lighter or other flame source

Ingredients

— 1/2 shot Amaretto
— 1/2 shot 151-proof rum
— 1/2 pint of lager beer

Procedure

— Fill half of shot glass with Amaretto, top with 151 Rum
— Ignite shot glass mix
— Pick up shot glass by sides, drop (bottoms first) into pint glass and chug
— Irish Carbomb (also known as Belfast Carbomb or just Carbomb)

Irish Carbomb

The Guinness beer and Irish Cream Liqueur will curdle together as soon as they make contact. The Irish Carbomb should be completely drunk before the drink has completely curdled. If done correctly, an Irish Carbomb should taste chocolatey.

Ingredients

— Guinness beer

— 1/3 shot of Irish Cream Liqueur such as Bailey's Irish Cream or Emmets Classic Cream
— 2/3 shot of Jameson Irish Whiskey

Directions

— Fill glass with half a pint of Guinness Beer.
— Combine Irish Cream and Jameson in a shot glass.
— Drop the shot (including the shot glass) into the glass of beer.
— Immediately drink the mix.

Jimmy&Guinney

Jimmy&Guinney is an Alcoholic Drink consisting of a proper Pint of Guinness and a double Shot of Jameson in a Whiskey snifter glass.

Lager and Lime

An English drink, most popular in hot weather. It is generally made by adding lime cordial, the most common brand being Rose's, to a pint glass and then topping up with lager.

Ordering a lager and lime without specifying the brand of lager will likely result in the cheapest lager being used, for example Carling Black Label, Foster's Lager or Carlsberg, rather than a more expensive brand such as Stella Artois or Kronenbourg.

The origins of the drink are unclear. One theory suggests that the combination was developed by 18th century sailors mixing together their rations of beer and lime cordial (the latter for its vitamin C content to protect against scurvy) in order to disguise the taste of either low-quality or spoiled beer.

Lolita

A Lolita (named after the eponymous novel by Nabokov) is a cocktail made from a mixture of beer, fresh lemon juice, a good shot of gin and ice cubes. It is a very refreshing long drink invented in France by sailors in the early 1980's.

Mickey Mouse

The Mickey Mouse is a cocktail that is apparently popular somewhere.

Ingredients

— 3 oz Tomato juice

— 1 dash Lemon juice

— 1/2 tsp Worcestershire sauce

-- 2-3 drops Tabasco sauce

— 1 wedge Lime

— Ice Cubes

Recipe

Shake all ingredients (except lime wedge) with ice and strain into an old-fashioned glass over ice cubes. Add salt and pepper to taste. Add the wedge of lime and serve.

Radler

A Radler is an alcoholic beverage consisting of equal parts of lager beer and lemonade. In Northern Germany, it is also known as an Alster (short for "Alsterwasser") or Potsdamer. In German, or at least its Bavarian dialect, Radler literally means cyclist.

- — In the Bavarian state of Germany, a mix of Weißbier (wheat beer) and lemonade is called a Russ.
- — Similar cocktails of beer and lemonade are known in England as a shandy and in France a panaché.
- — A New Zealand brewery Monteith's brew a beer called Radler. It has a distinct lemon and lime flavour to it, which makes it easy to drink for those who don't like the bitterness of beer, and often considered more thirst quenching than the average beer.

Radler was invented by the Munich gastronomer Franz Xaver Kugler when in September 1922 approximately 13,000 cyclists visited his tavern. On this particular day his beer started to run out, so he mixed the remaining beer with lemonade and pretended he created the Radler especially for the cyclists so that they could drive home without the risk of falling off their bicycles. During the summer months, Radler is still very popular in Bavaria and the rest of Germany, due to its reputation of being a thirst-quencher.

Shandy (Shandy Gaff)

A shandy (shortened form of shandygaff) is a cocktail made from a mixture of beer (often ale) and a non-alcoholic beverage. The non-alcoholic beverage is usually sparkling lemonade in Europe and ginger ale in the Caribbean. The proportions of the two ingredients are adjusted to taste, normally half-and-half, although shandy sold in tins is typically much weaker, around 1 part beer to 10 parts lemonade.

- — A variant on this is the "lager top" in which a small measure of lemonade is added to a pint or half-pint of lager. In some areas, tomato juice is mixed with beer as a cocktail.

— In Bavaria, a mix of helles Bier (lager) and lemonade is called a Radler (the German word for bicyclist), as opposed to a mix of Weißbier (wheat beer) and lemonade, which is called a Russ, short for Russian.

— Often a non-alcoholic beer is used, so that the drink has no alcoholic content and is therefore popular among children.

In Ireland a half and half of fizzy orange and lemon (no alcohol) is quite popular and commonly referred to as Rock Shandy. The Cantral & Cochran Group also market an Orange and Lemon drink under the brand Club Rock

Snakebite

The snakebite is a cocktail made from lager and cider. The basic snakebite is a mixture of equal parts of lager and cider (or alternatively a one third-two third mix), typically served in pint or half-pint servings. It has a reputation of being a "hard" drink, but the appeal of the drink seldom lasts into maturity and it is predominantly drunk by late adolescents.

In the snakebite and black (also known as snakebite, black, Purple nasty, Snakey B or diesel) variation, a shot of blackcurrant cordial is added before mixing in the beer and cider. Alternative variations can be made by using Benedictine or green Chartreuse liqueurs instead of the crème de cassis, while students may favour the cheaper blackcurrant squash.

There is a far more potent version of snakebite known by many names (such as deadly snakebite, hard snakebite, or super snakebite). This is made by combining a super lager with an ABV of at least 8% with a cheap cider such as White Lightning.

The resulting concoction will get the drinker very drunk very quickly, but also has a very strong taste and if drunk with any regularity, will combine the powers of super lager with those of cheap cider: at the very least, the hangover the following morning will be extremely unpleasant.

Cocktails with Bourbon

Bourbon County Cowboy

Bourbon county cowboy is a cocktail made of 2 oz. Bourbon whiskey | Bourbon and 1/2 oz. light cream, shaken with ice and strained into a cocktail glass.

Dixie Dew

Dixie Dew is a cocktail made of

— 2 oz Bourbon

— 1/2 tsp Creme de Menthe (white)

— 1/2 tsp Triple Sec

Shake all the ingredients in a shaker with ice. Strain into a cocktail glass. Serve.

Manhattan

A Manhattan is a cocktail made with rye whiskey or bourbon, vermouth (proportions vary from a "sweet" 1:1 to a "dry" 4:1), and a dash of bitters, stirred with ice and strained into a cocktail glass, garnished with a Maraschino cherry with a stem.

The bitters are omitted by many barmen unless specifically requested. Sometimes juice from the cherry jar is added to the cocktail to add sweetness and colour. Some recipes call for substituting orange bitters for the Angostura bitters.

Manhattans are traditionally made with brandy rather than bourbon in Wisconsin and a few surrounding areas.

Therefore, it is crucial to specify your preferred spirit when traveling in these areas to avoid disappointment. The following are variations on the classic Manhattan:

— A Rob Roy is made with Scotch whisky as its principal ingredient.

— A Perfect Manhattan is made with equal parts sweet and dry vermouth.

— A Cuban Manhattan is a Perfect Manhattan with dark rum as its principal ingredient.

— A popular Florida option consists of a lime instead of the cherry, bitters, and dry vermouth.

— A Latin Manhattan is made with equal parts of white rum, sweet and dry vermouth, and a splash Maraschino cherry juice, served up with a twist.

Mint Julep

The Mint Julep is a mixed alcoholic drink, or cocktail, distinctive to the southern U.S., and well-known as the official drink of the Kentucky Derby. Keeping a Mint Julep cold while drinking it was the reason the drinking straw was invented. The following is a sample recipe for one mint julep:

— Several to a few dozen mint leaves

— 3 to 5 oz. (90 to 150 mL) of Kentucky bo .rbon

— 1 tsp. (5 mL) of granulated sugar

— 2 tsp. (10 mL) of spring water

— Shaved or crushed ice

In a small bowl or glass muddle the mint, sugar, and water. Once the sugar is well dissolved, and the mixture has a good mint smell, stir in the bourbon. Pack a separate cup—preferably silver or pewter, but a highball will do—with crushed ice. Strain the bourbon mixture into the cup with the ice. Garnish with a sprig of mint, and serve with a drinking straw. Some tips for success:

— Strain well. Try to avoid getting any of the crushed mint in the final concoction.
— Use fresh mint. Four or five large spearmint leaves work well. Most other mints have smaller leaves, adjust accordingly.
— Instead of using sugar and water, use premixed sugar syrup. This helps avoid leaving grains of sugar in the drink.
— The mint, bourbon, and sugar can be pre-mixed in larger quantities, but always pour it over the ice immediately before serving.

Here are the directions for making a Southern Style Mint Julep:

Ingredients

— 5-6 sprigs mint
— 1 tsp. powdered sugar
— 2 tsps. water
— 2 1/2 oz bourbon

In a silver mug or collins glass, dissolve the powdered sugar with water. Then fill the glass with finely shaved ice. Next add the bourbon. Stir these contents until the glass is heavily frosted. Add more ice if necessary. Decorate the drink with sprigs of fresh mint so that the tops are about two inches above the rim of the glass.

Cocktail with Brandy or Cognac (drink)

B & B

B and B is a type of cocktail, made from equal parts brandy and Benedictine. The brandy is floated on top of the Benedictine in a cordial glass without mixing. B and B is also a ready-mixed drink, again of equal parts brandy and Benedictine, produced and bottled by the makers of Benedictine liqueur. Its alcohol content is 40% by weight. It is generally drunk either straight, on the rocks, or diluted with tonic water.

Belfast Bomber

Belfast bomber is a cocktail made with Brandy and Baileys Irish Cream; one measure of each is the usual mix. The Baileys must be poured first into the glass and the brandy second. Doing the opposite will cause the Baileys to curdle.

Blacksmith

Ingredients

— One part Brandy
— One part Drambuie
— One part Kaluah

Brandy Alexander

Brandy Alexander is a sweet brandy-based cocktail popular during the early 20th century. In older works, it can sometimes be found called a "Panama".

Recipe

— 1.5 oz brandy
— 1 oz Dark Creme de Cacao
— 1 oz half and half (or vanilla ice cream)
— 1/4 teaspoon powdered nutmeg

In a shaker half filled with ice cubes, add the Brandy, the half and half and the Creme de Cacao. Shake well. Pour into cocktail glass. Garnish with the grated nutmeg.

Brandy Cocktail

One recipe for making a brandy cocktail follows.

Ingredients

— 2 oz Brandy

— 1/4 tsp Sugar syrup

— 2 dashes Bitters

— 1 twist of Lemon peel

Mixing instructions

Stir all ingredients (except lemon peel) with ice and strain into a cocktail glass. Add the twist of lemon peel and serve.

Bull's Milk

A Bull's Milk is a cocktail. It consists of:

— 1 oz light rum

— 1 1/2 oz brandy

— 1 cup milk

A pinch of sugar, nutmeg and cinnamon is added.

Rolls Royce

A Rolls Royce cocktail is made of 1 1/2 oz. gin, 1/2 oz. each sweet vermouth and dry vermouth, and 1 tsp. Benedictine, stirred with ice and strained into a cocktail glass.

Sidecar

The Sidecar is a cocktail made of.

— 2 ounces brandy

— 1 ounce lemon juice

— 1 ounce Cointreau or triple sec

Shake or stir with ice. Strain into a cocktail glass. Sometimes, a small extra portion (the "sidecar") is served in a shot glass in addition to the portion served in the cocktail glass. The rim of the glass is sometimes coated in sugar in a manner similar to the salt on a margarita glass.

The Sidecar was originally invented at a bar in Paris for one of the patrons who was fond of arriving driven in a motorcycle sidecar. According to Embury, the original Sidecar had several more ingredients, which were refined away. A Sidecar according to Embury, a connoisseur of cocktails rather than a bartender, is simply a Daiquiri with brandy as its base rather than rum, and with Cointreau as the sweetening agent rather than sugar syrup. He recommends the same proportions (8:2:1) for both, making a much less sweet Sidecar.

Stinger

A stinger is a cocktail made with 1.5oz of brandy and 1/2oz of white creme de menthe. The ingredients are combined in a cocktail shaker and strained into a cocktail glass. The origins of this drink are murky, but it is mentioned in bartender's recipe books as far back as Tom Bullock's Ideal Bartender, published in 1917.

Cocktails with Gin

Aviation

The Aviation is a cocktail made of

— 2 ounces gin

— 1 ounce lemon juice

— 1 ounce maraschino liqueur

Shake or stir with ice. Strain into a cocktail glass. Serve with a cherry.

Maraschino liqueur is hard to find in the United States, and many bars do not stock it. Common brands of maraschino are Maraska, Luxardo and Stock. Other cherry-flavored liqueurs or the syrup from maraschino cherries should not be substituted, as they are much sweeter and have a very different taste.

Bronx Cocktail

A Bronx cocktail generally consists of:

— 1 oz vermouth

— 1 oz gin

— Juice of 1/4 orange

— 1 slice orange

Shake all ingredients (except orange slice) with ice and strain into a cocktail glass. Add the orange slice and serve. For a dry Bronx cocktail, use dry vermouth; for a Bronx golden cocktail, use half dry and half sweet, and add an egg yolk. The Bronx was supposedly invented by Johnnie Solon of the Waldorf-Astoria bar in Manhattan.

French 75

French 75 is a cocktail made from champagne and gin. The basic method is add to ice, gin, lemon juice, and sugar syrup in a boston glass. Shake and drain into champagne flute and top with champagne.

Gimlet(Cocktail)

The Gimlet is a cocktail typically made of

— 3 ounces gin

— 1/2 ounce bottled sweetened lime juice.

Stir well with ice, strain into a pre-chilled cocktail glass, and garnish with a lime wedge. A 1928 description of the drink was: "gin, a spot of lime, and soda". A 1953 description was: "a real gimlet is half gin and half Rose's Lime Juice and nothing else".

For the Vodka Gimlet, replace gin with vodka. As of the 1990s, maybe earlier, bartenders often answer requests for the gimlet with a vodka gimlet. Vodka gimlets were popularised by renowned proposition gambler and raconteur "Hong Kong" Freddie Wong, whose spirit of choice is quadruple-filtered Belvedere.

Surgeon Rear-Admiral Sir Thomas Desmond Gimlette served in the Royal Navy when cocktails started to become popular. A naval medical officer would certainly have had access to gin and lime juice.

Gin and Tonic

The gin and tonic is a cocktail made with gin and tonic water. The ingredients are usually mixed with a squeeze or slice of lemon or lime and served over ice. The proportions vary. While equal amounts are traditionally used, note that it is often made far weaker as a casual drink; typically 1 part gin to 3 parts tonic.

The cocktail was introduced by the British in India. Tonic water contains quinine, which was used to prevent malaria. Because the tonic water consumed to prevent malaria in the 19th century was extremely bitter, gin was added to make it more palatable. Although there is less medical use today for the consumption of tonic water, the gin and tonic remains a popular drink. Tonic water available today contains less quinine and is consequently less bitter (and usually sweetened). Because of this connection to warmer climates and its refreshing nature, this cocktail is more popular during the warmer months.

The gin and tonic has gained a central place in cultural and literary life, appearing as a bit part in numerous novels. One such example is in the Hitchhiker's Guide to the Galaxy series, where it is stated that each race in the galaxy has developed a drink that is pronounced the same, but spelled differently (such as jynantonnyx). The reason for this is one of the great mysteries of the universe.

Gin Fizz

Gin Fizz is a cocktail.

Ingredients

2 oz Gin, Juice of 1/2 Lemon, 1 tsp Powdered sugar, Carbonated water. Mixing instructions: Shake gin, juice of lemon, and powdered sugar with ice and strain into a highball glass over two ice cubes. Fill with carbonated water, stir, and serve.

Gin-Cassis Fizz

Ingredients

2 1/2 oz Gin, 1 1/2 oz Lemon juice, 1 tsp superfine Sugar, 4 oz Club soda, 1/2 oz Creme de cassis. Mixing instructions: In a shaker half-filled with ice cubes, combine the gin, lemon juice, and sugar. Shake well. Strain into a collins glass almost filled with ice cubes. Add the club soda. Stir well. Drop the cassis into the center of the drink.

Lady Finger

A Lady Finger drink is made as follows:

Ingredients

— 1 oz gin

— 1 oz kirschwasser

— 1/2 oz cherry brandy

— 1 oz lemon juice

— 1/2 tsp superfine sugar

Shake all the ingredients in a shaker with ice and strain into a cocktail glass.

Martini

The martini is a cocktail made with gin and vermouth. Over the years, the martini has become somewhat of an icon. H. L. Mencken once called the martini "the only American invention as perfect as the sonnet"; E. B. White called it "the elixir of quietude."

While variations are legion, a standard modern martini is made by combining approximately two and a half ounces of gin and one half ounce of dry vermouth with ice in a cocktail shaker or mixing glass. The ingredients are chilled, either by stirring or shaking, then strained and served "straight up" (without ice) in a chilled cocktail glass, and garnished with either an olive or a twist (a strip of lemon peel, usually squeesed or twisted to express volatile citric oils onto the surface of the drink).

Capers or cocktail onions are sometimes used as substitute garnishes. An onion-garnished martini is properly known as a Gibson. Another common but controversial variation is the vodka martini, which is prepared in exactly the same way as a standard martini, with vodka being substituted for gin as the base spirit. In the 1990s, the vodka martini supplanted the traditional gin-based martini in popularity. Today, when bar and restaurant customers order "a martini," they frequently have in mind a drink made with vodka.

Martini purists decry this development: while few object to the drink itself, they strenuously object to it being called "a martini." The martini, they insist, is a gin-based cocktail; this variation should be designated as such, with the name "vodka martini".

The origin of the martini is uncertain. By one widely accepted account, the martini is a descendant of the Martinez, an older, sweeter, but similar cocktail, which consists of (approximately) two ounces of sweet vermouth, one ounce gin (specifically, Old Tom gin, a sweetened variant), two dashes maraschino cherry liquid, and one dash bitters, shaken with ice, strained, and served with a twist of lemon.

The Martinez purportedly originated in California in the 1870s, probably either in San Francisco or in the town of Martinez. Some versions of this account are more specific, crediting the Martinez to Jerry Thomas, a famous and influential 19th century bartender working the Occidental Hotel in San Francisco in the late 1850s or 1860s.

Into a mixing glass place some cracked ice, two dashes of Orange bitters, half a jigger of (dry) French vermouth, and half a jigger of dry English gin. Stir well until thoroughly chilled, strain into a stem cocktail-glass, squeeze a piece of lemon peel over the top and serve with an olive. Other than the bitters and the ratio of vermouth to gin, this is remarkably similar to a modern martini cocktail. The reference to California is consistent, but other early martini history cites San Francisco rather than Los Angeles.

The martini was an established American cocktail at the beginning of the 20th century, but did not attain its pre-eminent status as the classic cocktail until later in the century. Perhaps paradoxically, Prohibition did a great deal to elevate the martini's stature. Americans' preferred tipple at that time—whiskey—requires skillful blending and long aging, whereas cheap but (marginally) drinkable "bathtub gin" is relatively easy to produce, so martinis were more readily available in the era of the speakeasy.

The Prohibition-era martini was quite "wet" by today's standards. With the repeal of Prohibition, and the ready availability of quality gin, the drink became progressively dryer. (A "dry" martini is one with relatively little vermouth. One might say that a "very dry" martini is essentially a glass of cold gin, though the ice will contribute some water to the final drink.) This trend toward dryness eventually reached fetishistic extremes, and became the source of a considerable body of martini anecdotes, wit, and lore.

One might prepare a martini by waving the cap of a vermouth bottle over the glass, or observing that "there was vermouth in the house once." Winston Churchill chose to forgo vermouth completely, and instead simply bowed in the direction of France, while General Patton suggested pointing the gin bottle in the general direction of Italy. Ernest Hemingway liked to order a "Montgomery", which was a martini mixed at a gin:vermouth ratio of 15:1 (these supposedly being the odds Field Marshall Montgomery wanted to have before going into battle).

In a classic bit of stage business in the 1955 play Auntie Mame sophisticated pre-adolescent Patrick Dennis offers a martini, which he prepares by swilling a drop of vermouth in the glass, then tossing it out before filling the glass with gin. Similarly, in the 1958 movie Teacher's Pet, Clark Gable mixes a martini by turning the bottle of vermouth upside-down before running the moistened cork around the rim of the glass and filling it with gin.

Coating the cubes is a method of adding the flavor of vermouth by pouring the vermouth in separately then pouring it out before pouring in the gin. Also, atomisers similar to those used for perfume were sometimes used to dispense a token amount of vermouth.

The martini's popularity waned in the health-conscious, wine-and-spritzer-drinking seventies, but resurged in the late eighties and nineties. During this "martini renaissance," vodka supplanted gin as the most commonly requested base spirit, and nouveau variations proliferated: the green apple martini, the chocolate martini, and so forth. Whether the more extreme variations of this era may truly be called martinis remains a topic of vigorous debate.

Western culture has created a virtual mythology around the martini. The classic martini of yore was stirred, "so as not to bruise the gin." W. Somerset Maugham declared that "Martinis should always be stirred, not shaken, so that the molecules lie sensuously one on top of the other," while James Bond from the Ian Fleming novels ordered his "shaken, not stirred", a drink properly called a Bradford.

In the novel Casino Royale, Bond's recipe is specified in more detail as made with three measures of gin (Gordon's was Bond's preference), one measure of vodka (Russian or Polish is preferred), and half a measure of Kina Lillet aperitif, shaken until ice-cold, and with a large, thin slice of lemon peel for garnish. By the second Bond novel, Live and Let Die, Bond was drinking vodka martinis, a trend that continued when 007 moved to the screen in 1962.

The concept of "bruising the gin" as a result of shaking a martini is an oft-debated topic. A shaken martini is different from stirred for a few reasons. The shaking action breaks up the ice and adds more water, slightly weakening the drink but also altering the taste. Some would say the shaken martini has a "more rounded" taste. Others, usually citing hard-to-track-down scientific studies, say that shaking causes more of a certain class of molecules (aldehydes) to bond with oxygen, resulting in a "sharper" taste.

Shaking also adds tiny air bubbles, which can lead to a cloudy drink instead of clear. Some martini devotees believe the vermouth is more evenly distributed by shaking, which can alter the flavor and texture of the beverage as well. In some places, a shaken martini is referred to as a "Martini James Bond".

The martini has become a symbol for cocktails and nightlife in general; American bars often have a picture of a conical martini glass with an olive on their signs. In Martini, Straight Up: The Classic American Cocktail, Lowell Edmunds, a classics professor and doyen of martini lore, analyses the cocktail's symbolic potency in considerable depth.

Martini variations

Many variations exist on the standard martini described above.

— A vodka martini (or vodkatini or kangaroo) is made the same way but with vodka instead of gin, and more often uses lemon rind as the garnish. This is the most common variation, and in fact is more popular than the original in most locations.

— An in-and-out martini is a very dry gin martini prepared by pouring a small measure of vermouth into a shaker, shaking it to coat the ice, and then pouring out and disposing of any remaining vermouth. The standard amount of gin is then shaken over this vermouth-tinged ice and served normally.

— A Churchill is made with dry gin, stirred, with an unopened bottle of vermouth waved above the shaker.

— An apple martini (also sour apple martini or appletini) is a vodka martini with an apple flavoring such as apple schnapps, sometimes with apple, lemon or lime juice, and is often garnished with a slice of Granny

Smith apple. Some people call this an "apple cosmopolitan".

- A dirty martini has some of the brine (at least a teaspoon) from the olive jar added. (FDR was partial to a dirty martini.)
- A naked martini is made without ice, but with the ingredients and glass chilled.
- A sweet martini is made with sweet red vermouth, and may be garnished with a maraschino cherry instead of an olive.
- A sake martini substitutes a dry, clear sake for the vermouth.
- A Gibson is a standard dry martini that is garnished with cocktail onions instead of olives.
- A tequila martini substitutes tequila for gin.
- An akvavit martini substitutes akvavit for gin.
- A gin salad is made like the ordinary martini but with three olives and two cocktail onions as garnish.

There are literally thousands of additional variants.

Sometimes the term "martini" is used to refer to other mostly-hard-liquor cocktails such as Manhattans, cosmopolitans, and ad-hoc or local concoctions whose only commonality with the drink is the cocktail glass in which they are served. Chefs with a more whimsical bent are even producing dessert "martinis" which are not a drink at all, but are merely served in martini glasses.

Negroni

The Negroni is a cocktail made of:

- 1 part gin
- 1 part Campari
- 1 part sweet vermouth

Shake the ingredients with ice. Strain into a chilled cocktail glass. Garnish with a twist of lemon. Common substitutes include vodka for the gin, dry vermouth for the sweet, or a twist of orange instead of lemon. According to the most popular origin story, the Negroni was invented in Florence, Italy in the early 1920s. It was named for Count Camillo Negroni, the man who invented it by asking a bartender to add gin to the Americano, his favourite drink. However, the word Negroni doesn't appear in English cocktail guides before 1947, so the drink's true origins are uncertain. The Negroni is an apéritif, or pre-dinner cocktail, intended to stimulate the drinker's appetite. There is also a variant, popular in Italy, named Negroni sbagliato, where the gin is substituted with spumante brut.

Satan's Whiskers

A Satan's Whiskers is a more florid variation of the Bronx cocktail:

— 1/2 oz gin
— 1/2 oz dry vermouth
— 1/2 oz sweet vermouth
— 1/2 oz fresh-squeezed orange juice
— 1/4 oz Grand Marnier
— 1 dash orange bitters

Shake all ingredients with ice and strain into a cocktail glass. Garnish with a twist of orange peel. The variation above has "straight" whiskers. For the "curled" variety, substitute 1/4 oz orange curaçao for the Grand Marnier, and increase the orange bitters to 1/4 oz.

Tom Collins

The Tom Collins is a cocktail and a variation on a Gin Sour. It is made of:

— gin

— lemon juice

— sugar

— splash of soda

Shake gin with lemon, sugar and ice. Pour into a Collins glass and top with soda. Garnish with an orange slice, lemon slice, or cocktail cherry. Garnishes vary by region. Nowadays, commercial "sweet and sour" is often used as a replacement for the sugar and lemon juice.

Wedding Belle

Wedding Belle cocktail is made with 1/3 dry gin, 1/3 Dubonnet, 1/6 orange juice and 1/6 cherry brandy, shaken with ice and strained into a glass.

White Lady

The White Lady is a cocktail made of

— 2 US fluid ounces (60 ml) gin

— 1 US fluid ounce (30 ml) lemon juice

— 1 US fluid ounce (30 ml) Cointreau or triple sec

Shake or stir with ice. Strain into a cocktail glass. It is essentially a Sidecar made with gin in place of brandy.

Cocktails with Rum

Banana Daiquiri

A banana daiquiri is a cocktail made of

— two parts light rum

— one part banana liqueur (Pisang Ambon)

— one part lime juice

— half a banana

— crushed ice

Mix the rum, banana liquor, lime juice, the banana and the ice in a blender. Strain into a cocktail glass. The banana daiquiri is known to be a favourite drink of Terry Pratchett, and appears in some of his Discworld novels.

Blue Hawaiian

A Blue Hawaiian is a cocktail made of:

— 1 part light rum

— 1 part blue curacao

— 2 parts pineapple juice

— 1 part cream of coconut

— 1 cup ice

— 1 cocktail cherry

— 1 piece of pineapple

Shake the rum, the blue curacao, the pineapple juice and the cream of coconut with the ice. Strain into a highball glass and garnish with a cherry and a piece of pineapple. The Blue Hawaiian was supposedly invented by Harry K. Yee while head barman of the Hawaiian Village Beach Resort & Spa in Waikiki, at the request of Bols marketers.

Brass Monkey

A Brass Monkey is a cocktail consisting of equal parts vodka, rum, and orange juice. It is thus essentially a screwdriver with rum added. Pulp-free orange juice is usually desirable for reasons of palatability, though freshly squeezed juice may also yield a good brass monkey. Dark rum is also preferable, since it is the mixing of the brown rum with the orange juice that produces the distinct brass-like coloration for which this drink is named.

An alternative cocktail, often attributed to the Beastie Boys track, is essentially a variation on a mimosa. It consists of three parts malt liquor and one part Sunny Delight. Typically Olde English 800 or St. Ides is used, and always in the forty-ounce bottle. The first quarter to third of the bottle is consumed, and then topped off with Sunny D, capped, inverted, and guzzled.

Cuba Libre

The Cuba Libre (Spanish for Free Cuba) was invented in Havana, Cuba around 1900. Patriots aiding Cuba during the Spanish-American War-and, later, expatriates avoiding Prohibition-regularly mixed rum and Coca-Cola as a cocktail and a toast to this West Indies island. The Cuba Libre (KOO-buh-LEE-breh) is a cocktail made of

— 3 ounces Coca-Cola

— lime wedge

— 1 ounce rum

Rub the rim of a highball glass with the lime. Fill with ice. Add rum and fill with Coca-Cola. Drop in the lime squeeze.

The world's most popular drink was born in a collision between the United States and Spain. It happened during the Spanish-American War at the turn of the century when Teddy Roosevelt, the Rough Riders, and Americans in large numbers arrived in Cuba. One afternoon, a group of off-duty soldiers from the U.S. Signal Corps were gathered in a bar in Old Havana. Fausto Rodriguez, a young messenger, later recalled that a captain came in and ordered Bacardi rum and Coca-Cola on ice with a wedge of lime.

The captain drank the concoction with such pleasure that it sparked the interest of the soldiers around him. They had the bartender prepare a round of the captain's drink for them. The Bacardi rum and Coke was an instant hit. As it does to this day, the drink united the crowd in a spirit of fun and good fellowship. When they ordered another round, one soldier suggested that they toast Por Cuba Libre in celebration of the newly freed Cuba. The captain raised his glass and sang out the battle cry that had inspired Cuba's victorious soldiers in the War of Independence.

The Cuba Libre gained further popularity in the U.S. after the Andrews Sisters recorded a song named after the drink's ingredients, "Rum and Coca-Cola." Coca-Cola and rum were both cheap at the time and this also contributed to the widespread popularity of the concoction. This drink was once viewed as exotic, with its dark syrup made, at that time, from cola nuts and coca.

Daiquiri

Daiquirí is a family of cocktails whose main ingredients are rum and lime juice. There are several versions, but those that gained international fame are the ones made in one of the most famous bars in the world: the Floridita, in Havana. The name Daiquirí is also the name of a beach near Santiago, Cuba, and a iron mine in that area. It is said that the cocktail was invented by an engineer that worked in that very mine, which explains the origin of the cocktail's name.

Daiquiri natural

Daiquirí Natural is the basic mix, that serves as the starting point to the more complex cocktails of the family:

— 1,3 oz light-dry (rum)

— 0,7 oz lime juice

— 1 teaspoon sugar

— crushed ice

Mix the ingredients in a shaker and serve.

Daiquiri floridita

This is the most common and famous version of this cocktail, allegedly it was invented by Constantino Ribalaigua Vert, barman and owner of the Floridita in the 1950s, whom Ernest Hemingway nicknamed El grande Constante. This recipe is also known as Daiquirí Frappé.

— 1,5 oz light-dry (rum)
— the juice of 1 lime
— 1 teaspoon sugar
— crushed ice
— 10 drops of Maraschino liqueur

Mix all the ingredients in a blender until ice is finely crushed and serve iced.

Frozen Daiquiris

A wide variety of alcoholic drinks made with finely pulverized ice are often called "frozen daiquiris". Although to purists most of these are not true daiquiris at all, use of this term to describe these drinks is common. Such drinks are often commercially made in machines which produce a texture similar to a smoothie, and come in a wide variety of flavors made with various alcohol or liquors.

Mai Tai

Mai Tai is an alcoholic beverage purportedly invented at the Trader Vic restaurant in Oakland, California in 1944. Trader Vic's amicable rival, Don the Beachcomber, claimed to have created it first in 1933 at his own newly opened little bar (later a famous restaurant) in Hollywood. The Beachcomber's recipe is far more complicated than that of the Trader's and tastes quite different.

"Maitai" is the Tahitian word for "good." An Internet search for references coupled with the word "rum" shows 40,600 hits for "Maitai" and 38,400 hits for "Mai Tai", so correct usage for this drink can apparently be either one word or two. The Trader Vic story of its invention is that the Trader created it one afternoon for some friends who were visiting from Tahiti.

Mojito

Mojito (pronounced mo-HEE-toe) is a traditional Cuban cocktail which became quite popular in the United States during the late 1890s.

Hemingway mojito

Ernest Hemingway was fond of the mojitos at La Bodeguita del Medio in Havana, though his recipe has no sugar.

— 3 parts light-dry rum

— 12 yerba buena or mint leaves

— ½ lime

— 2 dashes bitters

— simple syrup (can be made at home with equal parts sugar and water, boiled)

— crushed ice

The mint leaves should be crushed with a mortar and pestle. Mix everything together and serve.

Bacardi mojito

Rum producer Bacardi popularised an updated version of the drink in the early 2000s. It was featured in the action film Bad Boys II, and in 2002 was used in the James Bond movie Die Another Day.

In a cocktail shaker, mix:

— 2 shots light rum

— ½ shot of soda water

— 1 teaspoon simple syrup or sugar

— juice from half a lime

— 3 or 4 cubes of ice

Shake well until the sugar is dissolved and the mixture is chilled. Now add five whole mint leaves and two handfuls of ice. Shake the mixture just enough to bruise the mint leaves—about 5 seconds is fine; the leaves should remain mostly whole. Pour the contents of the shaker and the other ½ lime in a tall glass. Room should remain for another 3½ shots of soda water, which should be stirred in gently, to ensure that it does not lose its fizz.

Paradisus varadero mojito

Another recipe for mojitos from the Paradisus Varadero Resort:

— 1 1/2 ounces of rum (preferably Havana Club)

— Lime juice from one lime

— 3-4 teaspoons of sugar

— Mint

— Soda Water

— Ice

Combine lime juice, 4 teaspoons sugar, and a large sprig of mint in the bottom of a glass. Grind/bruise the mint leaves. Add plenty of ice, then add the rum, and top off with soda water.

Virgin mojito

Also very tasty is a fauxjito (pronounced foe-HEE-toe), a virgin (without the rum) version of the mojito.

Piña Colada

A Piña colada is a sweet cocktail. The name is from the Spanish words piña (pineapple) and colada (strained). The pulped or mashed pineapple is strained through a sieve. A non-alcoholic version is known as the Virgin Piña Colada. It was created in a bar on Calle Fortaleza, Old San Juan, Puerto Rico, by a man called Monchito in 1954.

Rum and Coke

Rum and Coke is a cocktail consisting of rum and cola. To make it, put some ice cubes in a glass; pour the rum and the cola over the ice; add a twist of lemon or lime.

— Common proportions are 50/50; or 2oz rum with a 12oz can of Cola.

— Rum (80 proof) and Coke is also the base of a Cuba Libre.

Tom and Jerry

A Tom and Jerry is a British mixed drink and also an American punch: an egg nog spiked with brandy and rum and served hot, usually in a mug. An early bartender's guide How to Mix Drinks was credited to "Jerry Thomas".

Cocktails with Vodka

Black Cossack

The Black Cossack is a cocktail made of :

— Guinness

— Vodka

White Russian

The White Russian is a sweet cocktail for many occasions. It was the favourite drink of 'The Dude' in The Big

Lebowski. It is making by mixing the vodka (preferably on ice) and top with milk or cream. A Black Russian is basically a White Russian without the cream.

Bloody Mary

Bloody Mary is a name used to refer to Queen Mary I of England because of her persecution of Protestants.

A Bloody Mary is a cocktail containing vodka and tomato juice, and usually other spices or flavorings such as Worcestershire sauce, Tabasco sauce, beef consomme or bouillon, horseradish, celery or celery salt, salt, black pepper, cayenne pepper, and lemon juice. Many bartenders jealously guard secret recipes for the drink. It is usually garnished with a celery stick and green olives, and is served in a tall glass often over ice. It is one of the few cocktails traditionally served in the morning, along with the Screwdriver and the Mimosa. If the drink is served without the vodka, it is called a Virgin Mary.

Greyhound

A greyhound is a cocktail consisting of 6 ounces of grapefruit juice and 1.5 ounces of vodka, mixed and served over ice. Salt the rim of the glass to turn it into a salty dog.

Harvey Wallbanger

The Harvey Wallbanger is an alcoholic drink or cocktail. According to legend, Harvey was a Californian surfer. After losing an important contest, he consoled himself with a screwdriver cocktail, but added a dash of Galliano liqueur. After several drinks, he tried to leave the bar, but unfortunately kept bumping into the furniture and walls. Harvey 'the Wallbanger' became his nickname and the famous drink was born.

Ingredients:

— Ice cubes

— 2 measures Vodka

— 3/4 measure Galliano

— 5 measures orange juice

— 1 slice of orange

Method:

Half-fill the shaker with ice cubes. Add the Vodka and orange juice, and shake well. Strain into an ice-filled highball glass. Gently float the Galliano on top, and garnish with the orange slice.

Kremlin Colonel

The Kremlin Colonel is a cocktail made from vodka, mint leaves, lime juice, and sugar syrup.

Long Island Iced Tea

A Long Island Ice Tea is a cocktail made with:

— 1/2 ounce vodka

— 1/2 ounce gin

— 1/2 ounce white rum

— 1/2 ounce Cointreau

— 1 ounce lemon juice

— cola

Build all ingredients in an ice tea glass, top with cola and garnish with lemon wedge.

Moscow Mule

Moscow Mule is a cocktail comprising of:

— 2 parts vodka (50ml)

— Fresh Lime juice

— Ginger Beer

— Lime

Ice , vodka, fresh lime juice placed in a boston glass. Shake and drain in a collins glass with ice lengthened with ginger beer.

Mudslide

The Mudslide is an alcoholic beverage also known as the Screaming Orgasm.

— 1 part Vodka or Amaretto

— 2 parts Bailey's Irish Cream

Rabid Dog

The Rabid Dog, Wsciekly Pies, is a cocktail that is currently popular in Poland.

— 1 part raspberry syrup

— 3 parts well chilled Polish vodka

— 2-4 drops of Tabasco sauce or a pinch of cayenne pepper

Fill 1/4 of a small shot glass (25 g) with raspberry syrup. Slowly pour vodka over it. The vodka should form a separate layer (use a small spoon to guide vodka to the surface of the syrup). Add drops of Tabasco or a pinch of Cayenne on top. Drink in one gulp.

Salty dog

A salty dog is a cocktail of vodka and grapefruit juice, served in a glass with a salted rim.

Sex on the Beach

Sex on the Beach is a variety of cocktail popular in the

United States. As with other popular cocktails, there are many varieties. One of the most popular versions contains:

— 2 oz. Vodka

— 1 oz. Peach schnapps

— splash of Orange Juice

— splash of Cranberry Juice

Soviet cocktail

Ingredients:

— 1 1/2 oz Vodka

— 1/2 oz Dry Vermouth

— 1/2 oz Amontillado Sherry

— Lemon peel

Shake all ingredients (except lemon peel) with ice, pour in a glass over ice cubes. Add the twist of lemon peel and serve.

Gimlet Cocktail

The Gimlet is a cocktail typically made of

— 2 ounces gin

— 2 ounces bottled sweetened lime juice (such as Rose's)

— 1 teaspoon sugar

Stir well with ice. Strain into pre-chilled cocktail glass. Sugar-frost rim of glass.

Grasshopper Cocktail

Ingredients:

— 1 oz Vodka

— 1 oz Creme de Menth (green)

— 1 oz Creme de Cacao (white)

Shake all the ingredients in a shaker with ice cubes and strain into cocktail glass.

Cocktails with Whisky

Boilermaker

A boilermaker is a cocktail made by pouring a shot of whiskey into a glass of beer. The shot and the beer are served separately, and you mix the two yourself by dropping the shotglass and its whiskey into the beer.

Dom Pedro

A Dom Pedro is an alcoholic milk shake, usually made with whiskey or Amarula. Typically: one shot of Irish whiskey, two spoons of vanilla ice cream, and a little bit of double cream whisked together, lightly topped with shavings of dark chocolate.

Horse's Neck

A Horse's Neck is an alcoholic drink. It is a highball made with whiskey (usually rye or bourbon) and ginger ale, with a long spiral of lemon peel draped over the edge of the glass.

Old Fashioned

The Old Fashioned is a cocktail.

MRecipe:

— 2 oz. whiskey or Bourbon

— splash of simple syrup

— bitters

— soda

Fill rocks glass with ice Add simple syrup, bitters, liquor, and soda Garnish with an orange slice and cherry For the "muddled" variant, muddle the orange slice and cherry in bottom of a rocks glass with simple syrup and bitters before adding the liquor and splash of soda.

Rob Roy Cocktail

A Rob Roy is a cocktail with a certain structural similarity to a Manhattan and also to the ubiquitous Martini.

Rusty Nail

A Rusty Nail is an alcoholic beverage made of 1.5 oz. of Scotch whisky and 1.5 oz. of Drambuie mixed and served over ice with a lemon twist garnish.

Sazerac

The Sazerac is one of the oldest known cocktails. To make a Sazerac, coat the inside of an Old Fashioned glass with a teaspoon or so of Herbsaint, Pernod or some similar pastis; swirl around until the inside is coated and discard the excess. To a mixing glass 2/3 filled with cracked ice add one teaspoon of simple syrup, 3-4 dashes of Peychaud's bitters and 2 to 2.5 ounces of rye whiskey; stir for thirty seconds. Strain into the pastis-coated glass. Garnish with lemon peel, making sure to twist it to express a coating of lemon oil onto the surface of the drink.

Simple syrup is preferred for convenience, and to avoid any undissolved sugar in your drink. If you're a traditionalist, before adding the ice to the mixing glass add a sugar cube and about a tablespoon of water, then the bitters, then muddle until the sugar is dissolved as much as possible. Then add ice and spirits; stir, strain and serve.

The original Sazerac cocktail was made with French brandy rather than whiskey, and was named after a specific brand of Cognac, Sazerac-du-Forge et fils. If rye whiskey is unavailable, Cognac makes a lovely Sazerac. Bourbon is not recommended, as it changes the character of the drink.

Cocktails with Wine

Bellini

Bellini is a simple cocktail that originated in Rome. It is an equal mixture of Champagne and peach juice, often served at celebrations.

Rossini cocktail

A Rossini cocktail is a combination of pureed strawberries and sparkling wine. A common recipe specifies one part strawberry puree for two parts wine. The strawberry mixture may be passed through a sieve in order to remove seeds, if desired.

7

EFFECTIVE BARTENDING

A bartender is the person behind a bar in a pub, tavern, inn, bar, or restaurant that serves beverages, both alcoholic and nonalcoholic alike. Their job is to mix and serve cocktails, beer, wine,shots, and other alcoholic beverages to the bar's clientele. In regions where tipping is the norm, bartenders receive a low base wage and earn most of their money through tips.

In the United States Bartenders are frequently considered the aristocracy of the working class, revered by the blue collar worker. There is a mythos about the trade; the abilities of a bartender are expected to go far beyond the obvious drink making and food serving. Bartenders (Barkeeps, drinkslingers or simply: "tenders") provide solace to the downtrodden drinking man, company for the lonely, entertainment for the bored and useful information to visitors.

For example a bartender might be called upon to recommend a restaurant for dinner, a theater for a show, the day's sports scores, the marital status of women lounging in the bar area, as well as a wide breadth of general trivia regarding stocks, cars, wine, sports, politics and history.

In some states within the USA, you may need to become certified before taking a bartending job. This is not true in all states, but it is best to learn the laws concerning your area. There are stiff penalties, fines and even jail time if you get caught serving alcohol to a minor. Also, there are thousands of drinks to learn. In some regions a drink may go by different names than in other regions. So, learning what your locals call a popular drink is the key. Also, keeping up with new drinks takes a person with a really superior memory.

Flair Bartending

Flair Bartending is the practice of entertaining guests, clientele, or audience with the throwing/juggling of bar tools (eg; shaker tins) and liquor bottles in tricky, dazzling ways. Used occasionally in cocktail bars, the action requires skill due to the dangers of glass breakage and possible burn (high alcohol spirit in contact with a lit candle or cigarette can ignite).

It has become a sought after talent among venue owners and marketers to help advertise a liquor product or the opening of a bar establishment. Competitions have been organised by liquor brands to attract flair bartenders, and some hospitality training companies hold courses to teach techniques of throwing and catching. Plastic bottles have been created for learning and practicing.

"Flair", or "freestyle bartending", as it may be called can be divided into two styles; working flair or competition flair. The difference between the two being the level of risk and complication of the tricks are higher for competitions. Good flair should be light hearted and entertaining while making actual, drinkable cocktails. It is a form of showmanship for confident cocktail bartenders that differs from the ideas behind mixology and drink-orientated, or service-minded bartending.

Tips for a Good Bartender

It doesn't matter how long someone has been a bartender, they can always use good bartending tips, because within the vast world of bartending, there are a lot of tips that can be offered. Anything that will help someone's performance is always a good thing. Flaming for instance, is one of the bartending tips that a lot of people would appreciate.

— Flaming liqueurs is awesome, but can also be extremely dangerous. Most liqueurs with high alcohol content are really easy to flame, and continue to burn even if the flame isn't visible. Bacardi 151 rum is a good example of flaming alcohol. Here are a few tips on flaming your liqueurs.

— Simply warm your liqueur up in a sauce pan and have a pre warmed cocktail glass ready. After heating the glass, pour the rest or other alcohols into the glass to warm. The glass can be heated over an element or a flame, but use caution to avoid contact with the glass and element or flame as the glass will break or char easy.

— When the alcohol has been heated, ignite it and add it to the alcohol in the glass. If done correctly, the alcohol in the glass will be warm enoug to flame also.

— When flaming liqueurs, be sure to keep any objects away from the glass. Flames can often shoot high up and ignite things in their way. If igniting liqueurs, use extreme caution and enjoy the fireworks.

— Something else associated with bartending tips that is always appreciated, is layering. Layering or floating liqueurs is one of the most difficult techniques in bartending.

— Although this bartending tip seems like a challenge, there is a very simple method that you can use. Each liqueur weighs differently and either floats or sinks when added to another.

— A lot of recipes are written with the heaviest liqueurs printed first. If all else fails, experiment and get used to the liqueurs that you most often use.

— To pour the liqueurs into the glass, simply use the rounded or back part of a spoon and rest it against the inside of the glass. Slowly pour down the spoon and into the glass.

— The liqueur should run down the inside of the glass and smoothly layer. This bartending tip takes practice, but can mastered by anyone.

— Make sure that the liqueurs are poured in order of their weight, starting with the heaviest first. The next thing that people tend to appreciate bartending tips with is shaking or blending drinks.

— This method is common with drinks containing fruit juices, cream, or eggs. In today's time, a blender is most often used to blend drinks, but the old fashioned shake method is usually the best.

— Fill the shaker to 2/3 with ice and add the ingredients. After adding the ingredients, cover the shaker and proceed to shake. This is usually done by shaking over your shoulder.

— Remove the cover and strain into the proper glass, allowing the drink to form a foamy head. Finish by garnishing and adding a straw.

— To assist you in understanding bartending words; A Taste of Texas offer you their Glossary of Bar Terms

And here are some more bartending tips for yourself and your bar.

— Even Professionals measures the ingredients. So don't guess to make a perfect drink every time; these are some Basic Bar Measures:

— One Normal Shot Glass= 1oz.

— Jigger = 1.5 oz-2 oz

— Pony = 1 oz

— Dash = 1/6 oz

— Teaspoon = 1/8 oz

— Always put ice in the glass or shaker before pouring ingredients. That way, the liquids are chilled as they are poured over ice.

— Serve cocktails icy cold! Pre-chill glasses in the refrigerator or let them sit in shaved ice before using. It makes drinks tastier!

— When the recipe calls for a twist of lemon peel, rub a narrow strip of peel around the rim of the glass. Then twist the peel so that one small drop will go into the drink. Then drop the peel.

— If you want more juice from lemons and oranges if you soak them in warm water.

— When you shake a drink that requires an egg, use an ice cube. It breaks up the egg and helps it blend into the drink.

— When the drink consists of clear liquids, STIR! If the drink has a carbonated drink (soda, ginger ale), stir gently to preserve the bubbly! SHAKE drinks that contain fruit juices, sugar, eggs, cream or other ingredients difficult to mix. Really SHAKE - don't just rock!

— A clean piece of wax paper rubbed on the rim of a bottle will prevent dripping when you pour!

— For a "sugar-frosted" glass, moisten the rim of a pre-chilled glass with lemon or lime and then dip into powdered sugar (before alcohol is poured).

The following are some of the basic bartending tips:-

Building: Pour one on top of the other, allowing them to mix. Most highball drinks are made this way. For example, for a Rum and Coke, you would put ice in the glass, add the rum, then add the coke. The carbonation in the soda allows it to mix naturally. You always add the liquor first, followed by the mixer.

Another example is a Tequila Sunrise. Fill the glass with ice, add the tequila, fill almost to the top with orange juice, then top with grenadine. This gives the drink it's "sunrise" appearance. There's no special pouring technique as there is with layering, but the order is often important.

Blending: Add the ingredients with ice into a blender and blend until smooth. This takes practice to get right. Too much ice and the drink seems weak, too little and it seems runny. Usually, the liquids should fill about 1/2 to 2/3 of the way up the ice.

Shaking: This requires a cocktail shaker, also referred to as a "Boston" shaker. You can use the type that come with a lid for a more elegant appearance, or you can use the metal mixing cup/pint glass combo for more speed and flexibility. Fill the shaker with ice, then add the ingredients. Shake (away from your guests to avoid a tip eliminating accident) and then pour into a glass. Typically drinks that are shaken are also strained.

Stirring: Fill a large glass (typically a pint glass) with ice, add the ingredients, stir with a bar spoon, and pour or strain into the final glass.

Straining: After shaking or stirring, straining simply means to pour the liquid, leaving the ice. This prevents the drink from becoming diluted over time. Classic examples of this include the Martini and the Cosmopolitan.

Layering: This takes practice to do properly. By gently placing one liqueur on top of another you can create a layered effect where the liqueurs don't mix. To do this, you can tilt the glass and slowly pour one liquor on top of another, or you can pour over the back of a spoon as well. Either way, the liquor on top has to be less dense than the liquor on the bottom or they won't stay separate. If you pour sloppily you can just set it refrigerator. The layers will separate themselves.

Making Simple Sugar Syrup: Simple syrup, also known as sugar syrup, can be made into a variety of thicknesses for a variety of different uses.

— Cooled thin syrup (3 parts water to 1 part sugar) is useful for brushing onto cakes to add a bit of extra sweetness and moisture.

— Medium-thick syrup (2 parts water to 1 part sugar) is great for adding sweetness to teas and coffees.

— Thick simple syrup (1 part water to 1 part sugar) is excellent for candying fruits and veggies.

Pouring and Serving Draught Beer

When pouring beer from a tap, open the faucet all the way with a quick, smooth motion by grasping the tap handle at its base. Pulling the tap handle at the top opens the faucet too slowly, and beer will draw foamy. At the beginning of the pour, tilt the glass slightly and don't let the glass touch the beer faucet. Then straighten the glass as you pour, and top it with a collar of ½ inch to 1 inch of foam.

To make sure your glasses are "beer clean," a three-sink cleaning system is ideal. The first sink is for washing the glasses, the second for rinsing, and the third for sanitising the glasses. If you have a two-sink system, use the first for cleaning the glasses and the second for sanitising.

— Make sure you always use cleaners and sanitisers specifically designed for cleaning beer glasses.

— When drying the glasses be sure to allow airflow inside the glasses. Usually best to use a drying rack.

— Before pouring beer be sure to rinse the glass with cold water whenever possible.

— Ways to check if your glasses are beer clean.

— Wet the inside of the glass and turn upside down. If the water drops stick to the side it is not "beer clean."

— Bubbles will not form on the sides of a glass that is not "beer clean."

— Lacing from the head will only form on the sides of a "beer clean" glass as well

These are a few more quick bartending tips to help you along the way:-

— A 1/2 oz. of liquor equals 1 count.

— If you are using a pourer on your bottles, to measure 1-1/2 oz. of liquor, count

— "1-1,000...2-1,000...3-1,000"

— As you pour. You will eventually be able to do it by eye with practice.

— Cocktails & other shaken/stirred drinks

— Fill shaker half-full of ice.

— Most shaken drinks that contain light cream can also be made as blended drinks, substituting vanilla ice cream for the light cream.

— To make blended drinks:-

  — It is always best to add your liquor(s) and juice(s) prior to adding the ice.

  — That assists with less ice melt that will only water down the drink and make a soupy, flimsy slush.

Also a good rule of thumb, each scoop of ice that goes into the liquor-filled-blender-pitcher equals roughly the number of drinks you wish to make.

— For Lowballs (drinks made in an old fashion or rock glass)

— Fill the glass about half-full of ice before pouring the drink.

— For Highballs

— Fill the glass with 2/3 of ice before adding liquor. Always pour liquor in before the mixer.

— Never stir drinks containing carbonated mixers until after the mixer has been added.

— Always keep fruit juices and other mixers refrigerated.

— Always use fresh fruit in fruit drinks, e.g. strawberry margaritas, banana daiquiris.

— Always be a responsible drinker/bartender.

— Above all never drink and drive

And here is a good bartending tip for being efficient:-

Bartending Tools

Some tools aid in bartending, while some are required. There are hundreds of different ones out there, while each one serves its own unique purpose. If you didn't have a bottle opener, you probably wouldn't be able to open most of the bottles within a bar.

This tool is required for any type of bar to operate.If you were to go into a bar during operation, you would see a lot of utensils being used by the bartender. The bartender knows how to use each one, and exactly how each it will benefit him.

— There are some implements, that don't really require usage, but will help the user out a lot. These types save a lot of time, and a lot of effort when properly used.

— The blender is an extremely essential bartending tool. While some bars operate without a blender, most have one. A blender saves a lot of time and work when drinks called for crushed or blended ice.

— All the bartender has to do is pop some ice into the blender, and within seconds he has what he needs to make the drink. The old traditional way will work, but it takes time.

— Glasses are required bartending items. Without a glass, you would have nothing to hold your drink. Glasses come in all different shapes and sizes, depending upon what you're drinking.

— Frosted glasses are excellent when drinking beer; they give the beer that fresh out of the fridge look and feel. A lot of bartending tools, come in different sizes and colours.

— The different look of these tools provides a certain look of fashion when using it around the bar. While the different colours don't really matter when using the tool, they make the look of it better when compared to a plain old white item.

— You could order bartending devices in sets, or separately. If ordering them in sets, you usually get many different tools within that specific set. This could save you a lot of money, when you compare the set with buying each piece by itself.

— Some tools can be quite expensive, but when sold in a set, the cost of expensive implements almost always seems to weigh itself out. There are a lot of places that deal with bartending tools.

— If you know a certain tool that you need, it's a good idea to see if it is sold in a set. Bartending tools are good to have, and make the environment of the bar work and look that much better.

The most important assets for any profession are the right tools. You need basic bar tools to mix, serve, and store your drinks. Whether you're stocking a home bar or working as a professional, your basic tools are a wine opener, cocktail shaker, measuring glass, and strainer.

Wine Opener

The best wine opener is a waiter's wine opener (Figure 1). It has a sharp blade, a corkscrew (also known as a worm), and a bottle opener. This wine opener can be found in most liquor stores or bar supply houses.

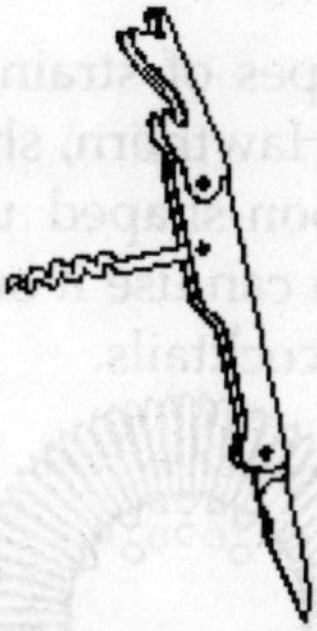

Figure 1. A waiter's wine opener

Cocktail Shaker

Two types of shakers are shown in Figure 2. The Boston shaker is the one that most professional bartenders use. It consists of a mixing glass and a stainless steel core that overlaps the glass. The Standard shaker usually consists of two or more stainless steel or glass parts and can be found in department stores or antiques stores. Many of these shakers come in different shapes and designs.

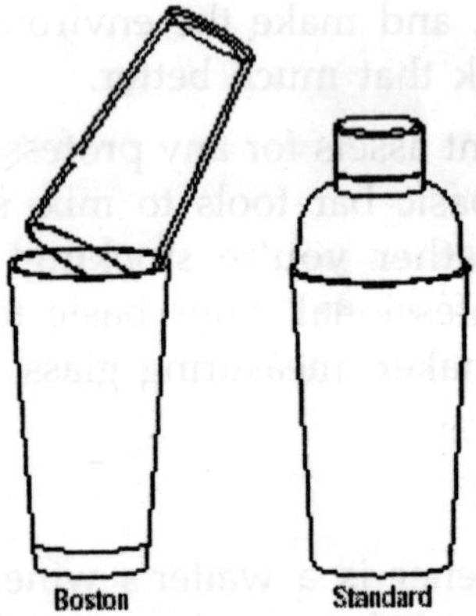

Figure 2. A Boston shaker and a Standard shaker

Strainer

A couple of different types of strainers are available, but the most popular is the Hawthorn, shown in Figure 3. The Hawthorn is a flat, spoon-shaped utensil with a spring coil around its head. You can use it on top of a steel shaker or a bar glass to strain cocktails.

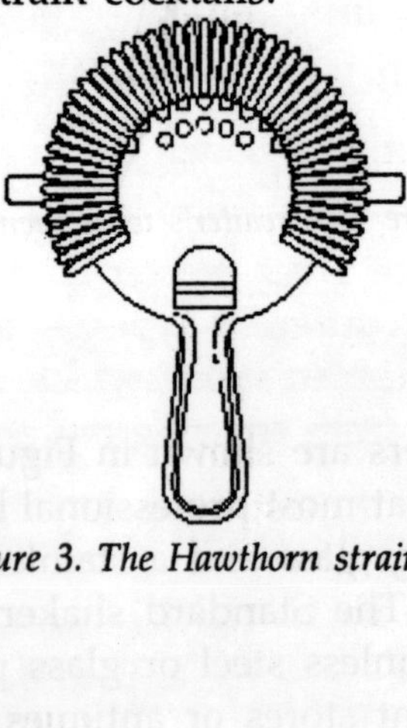

Figure 3. The Hawthorn strainer

Other Tools

Many of the following tools are shown in Figure 4

— *Bar spoon*: A long spoon for stirring cocktails.

— *Blender*: Many types of commercial or home blenders with various speeds are available. Always put liquid in first before switching it on when making a drink. This will save your blade. Some blenders (but not all) can be used to make crushed ice. Check with the manufacturer or buy an ice crusher.

— *Coasters or bar napkins*: Coasters prevent rings from developing on your bar and other tables. Napkins also help your guests hold their drinks.

— *Ice bucket*: Pick one that's large enough to hold at least three trays of ice.

— *Ice scoop or tongs*: A must for every bar. Never use your hands to scoop ice.

— *Jigger or measuring glass*: A small glass or metal measuring container that usually has a 1.2 oz. measurer on one side and a 2 oz. measurer on the other.

— *Knife and cutting board*: You need a small, sharp paring knife to cut fruit.

— *Large water pitcher*: Someone always wants water.

— *Muddler*: A small wooden bat or pestle used to crush fruit or herbs.

Pourer: This device gives greater control to your pouring. A variety of different types is available, including some with a lidded spout, which prevents insects and undesirables from entering the pourer.

— *Stirrers and straws*: Used for stirring and sipping drinks.

— *Large cups or bowls*: Used to hold garnishes, such as cherries, olives, onions, and so on.

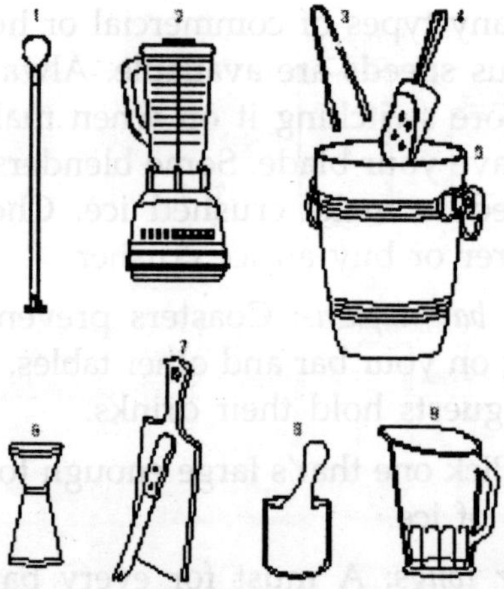

Figure 4: A collection of bar tools: (1) bar spoon, (2) blender, (3) tongs, (4) ice scoop, (5) ice bucket, (6) jigger or measuring glass, (7) knife and cutting board, (8) muddler, and (9) pourer.

Glassware

People generally expect certain drinks to be served in certain kinds of glasses. The problem is that there are more standard bar glasses than most people (and many bars) care to purchase. In any event, Figure 5 shows most of the glasses that you're ever likely to use to serve drinks. The glasses shown in Figure 5

— *Shot glass*: You can also use the shot glass as a measuring tool. It's a must for every bar.

— *Cocktail or martini glass*: Perfect for martinis, manhattans, stingers, and many other classic drinks, this glass is available in 3 to 6 oz. sizes.

— *White wine glass*: This glass is available in 5 to 10 oz. sizes.

— *Red wine glass*: This glass is also available in 5 to 10 oz. sizes. Note that the bowl is wider, allowing the wine to breathe.

Figure 5. Glasses, glasses, glasses

— *Champagne glass*: The bowl is tapered to prevent bubbles from escaping.

— *Rocks glass*: Also known as an old-fashioned glass, sizes vary from 5 to 10 oz. Use the 5 or 6 oz. variety and add plenty of ice.

— *Highball and collins glasses*: These are the most versatile glasses. Sizes range from 8 to 12 oz.

— *Cordial glass*: In addition to cordials, you can also use this glass for straight-up drinks.

— *Brandy or cognac snifter*: Available in a wide range of sizes, the short stemmed, large bowl should be cupped in hand to warm the brandy or cognac.

If you're planning on creating a bar at home or serving cocktails at a party, keep your glass selection small. You can simplify by using two types of glasses: a white wine glass and a red wine glass. Both are shown in Figure 5. These two glasses can be used for every type of cocktail plus beer and wine. Also, if you use these two glass shapes, cleaning and storing your glasses is less complicated.

8

Bar Equipment

Bar Stools

The type of seating you choose for your restaurant or bar must correspond with the length of time you expect your customers to be seated. Fast-food or quick turn-around restaurants will not want to provide seating that encourages lounging and extended stays. Alternatively, a fine dining establishment should make sure they provide comfortable seating. There are different types of bar stools:

Wood Bar Stools and Wood Chairs

Wood furniture provides a clean look that will compliment the existing décor of most any dining space. Wood Bar Stools and wood chairs are sturdy, easy to clean, and require little to nc maintenance. Shop our selection of wood bar stools and wood chairs for the best variety of wood furniture styles and finish colours.

Upholstered Wood Bar Stools and Upholstered Wood Chairs

Upholstered wood furniture provides moderate comfort to your customers. Upholstered wood bar stools and upholstered wood chairs allow you to bring more colour into your restaurant or bar since many of our upholstered wood furniture pieces are available in a variety of upholstery colours. Vinyl upholstered furniture is easy to clean and maintain. Shop our wide selection of upholstered wood bar stools and upholstered wood chairs.

Metal Frame Bar Stools and Metal Frame Chairs

Metal frame bar stools and metal frame chairs present a modern look to your restaurant or bar. Metal frame bar stools and metal frame chairs come in a variety of styles and upholstery options. Metal furniture is easy to clean and is very durable to everyday wear and tear.

Lounge Seating

Lounge chairs and lounge bar stools offer deluxe, comfortable seating. Lounge chairs and lounge stools are ideal for restaurants or bars that would like to encourage their customers to stay for longer periods of time. Lounge seating is available in a variety of upholstery colours in plain, tufted and channeled styles. Solid Chrome or Brass accents and bases complete the look of the lounge chairs and lounge bar stools.

Nostalgic 50's Bar Stools and Dining Chairs

Create a feeling of nostalgia in your restaurant or bar with retro, 50's styled bar stools and dining chairs. Heavy duty bar stools reflect the 50's era with Chrome frames and shiny vinyl upholstery. The nostalgic dining chairs feature unique detailing with Chrome frames, tufted upholstered backs and two-toned vinyl upholstery.

Booths

Booth seating is available with wall-mount frames and island frames. Booths are available with wood, laminate or upholstered seats. Laminate and wood booths are easily maintained and ideal for quick-turn around restaurants. Upholstered booths offer comfortable seating to customers that may have a longer wait for their meal to arrive. High-back booths offer a considerable amount of privacy to your customers, which will bring an intimate atmosphere to your restaurant or bar.

Outdoor Furniture

Move your customers outdoors for dinner with outdoor furniture. Choose from a variety of teak outdoor furniture, aluminum outdoor furniture, wicker outdoor furniture and durable resin outdoor furniture. Mosaic tables and mosaic chairs make a colourful addition to your outdoor seating area. Mosaic outdoor furniture features hand-made stained glass table tops and chair seats with powder coated, heat treated wrought iron bases and frames.

Stack Chairs and Folding Chairs

Furniture that allows for stacking or folding is ideal for banquet facilities and multi-purpose rooms. Stack chairs are useful in areas with minimal storage, and are easy to transport. Stack chairs are often referred to as banquet chairs, as they are most commonly used in banquet halls and multi-purpose dining facilities. Folding chairs are a good idea for providing additional seating and are generally cost-effective.

Table Tops and Table Bases

Choose a customised table for your restaurant with mix-and-match table tops and table bases. Choose a table base that will best suit your needs. Standard height table bases measure 28″ in height and stand-up height table bases measure up to 42″ in height. Once you have chosen a table base choose a table top. Serv-U offers a wide variety of laminated table tops, solid wood table tops, wood edge table tops, metal edge table tops, and aluminum table tops.

Youth Furniture and High Chairs

It is important to provide safe and reliable seating for infants and children that eat in your restaurant. Wood high chairs are sturdy, stackable, and easy to clean. Booster seats are available in a variety of colour choices. It may be wise to purchase the optional safety strap for your booster seats to ensure the booster seat is secured to your dining chairs.

Purchasing Equipment

Purchasing restaurant equipment does not need to be difficult. When purchasing commercial kitchen equipment it is wise to consider the following: safety features, quality, efficiency, any warranty and service plans, the reputation of the manufacturer, and all short- and long-term costs associated with your purchase.

Consider Quality

Many restaurant owners gauge the quality of restaurant equipment by the reputation of the manufacturer. In many instances a well respected brand of restaurant equipment has earned its reputation due to the exceptional value and quality of its products. It is commonly assumed that a name-brand piece of restaurant equipment will outperform that of its un-named competitor. This may not always be the case. Also, purchasing restaurant equipment by an un-named manufacturer may be less expensive.

Consider Cost

A restaurant owner's decision to purchase new restaurant

equipment should always be based on more than the initial cost of the unit. The buyer should weigh the total costs by short- and long-term considerations. In most cases new restaurant equipment is more energy efficient to operate than older restaurant equipment. Over time this will allow the restaurant owner to save money on utility costs. The warranty and service plan included with the purchase of a new unit of restaurant equipment may eliminate or reduce maintenance and service costs.

A great way to reduce costly repairs once a warranty or service plan has expired is to practice preventative maintenance and have your restaurant equipment serviced regularly. A new unit of restaurant equipment will include the latest technology and safety features. This will increase the efficiency of your kitchen and bring added safety to your employees.

Consider Your Needs

One way to determine the restaurant equipment needed to effectively and efficiently operate your restaurant is to create a work-flow chart for each item on your menu. Keep track of all restaurant equipment used to make each item on your menu. Be sure to take special notice of the restaurant equipment items used most frequently in the preparation of your menu items. It may be wise to invest more time and money in the purchase of these heavily used commercial cooking equipment units.

Consider the Investment

Most importantly, consider the purchase of your restaurant equipment as an investment. The success of your restaurant relies on your restaurant kitchen's ability to produce a quality product. The quality of your product relies on consistent and positive performance of your restaurant equipment. Experienced restaurant owners know that unreliable restaurant equipment will hurt their bottom line in more ways than one.

Other Bar Equipments

Back Bar Coolers

Back bar coolers should be placed behind the bar and will typically have 2-3 doors. Back bar coolers can be ordered with a stainless steel countertop or a galvanised top. Back bar coolers are available with solid doors and glass doors. For a multi-purpose unit choose the combination back bar cooler and beer dispenser by True. This unit features a direct draw beer dispenser built in to the back bar refrigerator.

Bar Blenders

Bar blenders allow for higher profits by extending the menu including frozen drinks, ice cream drinks or smoothies. When choosing bar blenders, consider the volume of drinks needed at peak time. High capacity bar blenders can crush a ½ gallon of ice in 3 seconds! Bar blenders containers are available in 32 Oz., 48 Oz., or ½ gallon capacities. Programmable bar blenders and drink stations increase drink consistency and allows operator to complete other tasks. Sound enclosures and in-counter bar blenders reduce the noise from powerful motors.

Bar Sinks

Bar sinks are available in a variety of configurations. Many bar sinks are designed as modular units so you can customise your work space exactly to your specifications. Drop-in bar sinks are great for custom applications. Look for a variety of bar sink units at Serv-U, many bar sink units are available in different depths and widths, to ensure a proper fit with your existing back bar equipment.

Beer Dispenser

Beer dispensers can accommodate one to five different kegs of beer at the same time. Beer dispensers are available in Black vinyl, Woodgrain vinyl and stainless steel. A club top direct draw beer dispenser has a shelf area at the back of the unit, plus sliding lids for quick access to the storage area. A one keg direct draw beer dispenser will hold 1/4 or 1/2 barrel kegs.

Beer Faucets

Choose from Chrome beer faucets, Brass beer faucets, stainless steel beer faucets and Black plastic beer faucets. Quick action stout faucets are perfect for low carbonated ales and stouts. Choose the beer faucet that will work best for your bar or restaurant.

Beer Line Cleaning

Beer line cleaning pumps are designed for use with direct draw and short run beverage systems. Choose from a manual cleaning system or an automatic, heavy duty model designed for larger systems or longer runs. Keep your beer line clean to ensure your customers receive a quality, fresh-tasting product from your bar.

Beer Merchandisers

Beer merchandisers come in a variety of shapes and sizes. Beer merchandisers are great for outdoor use and make transporting large quantities of beer and packaged beverages easy. Choose a beer merchandiser that will accommodate packaged beverages or a 1/4 gallon to 1/2 gallon size keg. Some beer merchandisers will hold multiple kegs, while most will hold one keg.

Beer Pumps

There are several different types of beer pumps available. Choose from a variety of picnic pumps and push pumps. Some beer pumps come with a beer dispensing hose, while other beer pumps have a beer faucet built onto the beer pump.

Beer Taps

Beer taps are available with wing handles and lever handles. Lever handle taps feature a snap-down handle that is safe, fast and easy to use. Wing handle taps operate easily with a quarter turn of the plastic handle.

Beer Towers

Choose from several beer towers for your bar. Beer towers are available with single, double or triple faucets. Many dome draft beer towers are available with up to six faucets, and also feature decorative accents to add flair to your bar.

Bottle Coolers

Choose a frosty brew bottle cooler from Beverage-Air® for high volume and fast pull-down applications. True® bottle coolers include adjustable bin dividers and a built-on bottle opener and cap catcher.

Brass Rail

Quality commercial grade brass railing and polished stainless steel railing are ideal for balcony and stair rails, dance bars, bar rails and guard rails. Solid brass or polished stainless steel bar rails and fittings are sturdy, attractive and extremely durable.

CO_2 Regulators

Single and double gauge CO_2 regulators feature a forged brass body, self-aligning spring plate and relief valve spring. You should monitor the CO_2 regulators to ensure applied operating pressures remain constant (10-12psi/lbs).

Drip Trays

Drip trays are great for catching spills from beer draft towers. Many counter top drip trays feature a threaded drain fitting so you do not need to empty the trays throughout the evening. Counter top dump trays sit on top of the bar and no drain is required, however these dump trays will need to be emptied throughout the evening, as they become full.

Glass Washers

Glass washers are an easy and efficient way to wash and clean bar glassware. Many glass washers feature instant installation and require no plumbing. Glass brushes are an easy solution for bars that do not want to purchase a glass washing machine. Glass brushes feature a sturdy plastic base with rubber suction to firmly hold to the bottom of the sink. Brushes for all glass washers are replaceable.

Ice Caddies

An ice caddy provides a safe method for transporting ice. Many ice caddies feature a sliding lid to help reduce the risk of cross contamination. Choose an ice caddy with casters for easy transportation of ice.

Juicers/Drink Mixers

Choose from manual juicers or electric juicers. Spindle mixers are great for mixing ice cream dinks, smoothies, or any other thick drink. A juicer allows you to make drinks with fresh fruits. Juicers are great for smoothie bars and restaurants serving breakfast and/or brunch items.

Portable Bars

Portable bars are great for banquet halls and rooms, or for taking a party outdoors. All portable bars come with locking casters for ease of mobility from room to room. Portable bars feature storage areas, speed rails and ice bins.

Speed rails

Speed rails accommodate a variety alcohol bottle sizes. Stainless steel speed rails are durable and used in most bars. Speed rails are typically mounted directly to the bar sink.

Wine racks

Countertop wine racks will help you sell more wine by displaying the product for customers. Choose from different sizes and metal finishes when choosing your wine rack. Each wine rack can accommodate up to six, twenty-one or forty-five wine bottles.

Wine Refrigerator

A wine merchandiser can hold a total wine bottle capacity of 50 bottles. Wine merchandisers include a lighted four-colour "Wine Cellar" sign. The interior floor of the unit can be used to merchandise liter bottles, and the top shelf can be used to merchandise packaged beverages. The specially designed wine bottle shelves allow for proper horizontal storage of wine bottles.

Ashtrays

Restaurants and bars permitting smoking should have plenty of ashtrays on hand to accommodate customers. Choose ashtrays that will be most effective for your restaurant or bar by choosing glass ashtrays, plastic ashtrays, metal ashtrays or disposable ashtrays. It is also a good idea to place smoking receptacles near the entrances and exits of your restaurant and bar so customers may properly extinguish and dispose of all cigarette butts. Many outdoor smoking receptacles will accommodate up to 3,000 extinguished cigarettes and nearly all are weather resistant and flame retardant.

Bar Knives

Bar knives and bar tools are essential for preparing drink garnishes such as lemons, limes, oranges, mint leaves and olives. A forked bar knife is a useful tool that will allow bartenders to safely retrieve condiment items such as cherries or olives from jars and will also cut and slice condiment items. A lemon or lime peeler will easily allow a bartender to peel and zest any type of citrus fruit.

Bar Mats and Shelf Liner

Bar matting improves airflow and moisture drainage when used with wet bar supplies. Interlockable bar matting allows for layout changes and can be trimmed to fit into the existing spaces of your bar. Shelf liner is great for glassware storage or dinnerware storage.

Bar Trays

Smaller round bar trays are ideal for bartenders and

servers that need to maneuver through groups of people. Cork lined trays and non skid bar trays are great for transporting beverages and appetizers that could easily spill or slide off the tray. Some bar trays feature a rim or lip around the edge of bar tray to prevent spill from running over the edge of the tray and onto a customer.

Bottle Openers and Corkscrews

While a bottle opener or a corkscrew may seem like a simple purchase, these items will undoubtedly get used very frequently behind almost every bar. Wall mount bottle openers are perfect for behind the bar use, your bartenders and servers will always know where to find a bottle opener. Some varieties of corkscrews and wine bottle openers can also be mounted to a wall or counter for security and extra leverage.

Cocktail Shakers

The cocktail shaker is typically a bartender's most useful tool. Most cocktail shakers are stainless steel 3-piece shakers, and typically include a strainer top and a jigger cap. Many bartenders feel stainless steel cocktail shakers are best, since they chill a drink more quickly than glass cocktail shakers. Vinyl coated cocktail shakers are constructed of stainless steel with a durable coating of vinyl to give the bartender a dry, sure grip.

Drain Trays

Drain trays are available with or without drain fittings. Most drain trays are composed of stainless steel or brass, and feature either a metal grid or a polystyrene grid.

Ice Scoops

Ice scoops are a very useful tool to have behind the bar.

Using an ice scoop to fill glasses reduces the risk of cross contamination. Choose an ice scoop that is tapered to facilitate pouring of ice into glasses. A slotted ice scoop will help to separate water from your ice.

Jiggers

A jigger is a dual sided measure cup, and comes in extremely handy behind the bar. Use a jigger when making mixed drinks to ensure you have the proper proportions of each ingredient.

Liquor Pours

Liquor pours are great way to maintain portion control in your bar. Measured pours range in size from 7/8 oz. to 1 1/2 oz. Straight pours will allow an unlimited amount of alcohol to pour from the bottle. Metal liquor pours can dress up your bar with their bright and shiny chrome finish.

Plastic Drinkware and Disposable Drinkware

Polycarbonate drinkware and disposable barware are great for outdoor seating and locations where glass is not permissible. Polycarbonate glassware is durable, shatterproof and dishwasher safe. Disposable barware is made from rigid styrene plastic.

Bar Game Supplies

Pool tables and dartboards are a good source of entertainment for your guests. Cue sticks are available in solid ramin wood, solid hardrock maple, and hardrock maple with a fiberglass coating. Pool table lights add an authentic look to your bar. Choose from plastic shade pool table lights and metal shade pool table lights. Electronic dartboards programmed for 19-30 different dart games are a great alternative to standard dartboards.

Wine Chillers

Wine chillers and wine buckets will keep your customers' wine chilled for the duration of their stay. Double wall wine coolers provide insulation that chills wine at the proper temperature for up to three hours. A genuine marble wine chiller will keep wine cold for 60 minutes. Champagne buckets and wine buckets provide an elegant look, and will typically hold up to two bottles of wine.

9

CATERING OF ALCOHOL

Alcohol is central to catered events. Without it, a party is simply not a party. As a guest, liquor service looks easy. But with this service comes responsibility, by-law and liability issues. Hosts and caterers alike are bound by strict obligations, so in essence, there is a lot of work behind this "social lubricant!" Guest safety is the ultimate issue, and certain procedures are put in place to protect guests at a party. If the event space is not licensed, then a Special Occasions Permit may be necessary (the only time it is unnecessary is if the party is being held on private property or is in a private space not accessible to the public).

If your event takes place in a mall, under a tent or at a public venue, you will need to apply for an "S.O.P." at least two weeks prior to the event at the LCBO located in the jurisdiction of the venue. You will be asked to designate someone who will ultimately be present and take responsibility for the event, and will be asked questions about the event itself (i.e. "Are persons under 19 years of age to be admitted?" and "Are you serving homemade wine/beer?"). If you are refused a Special Occasions Permit, you may not serve alcohol!

On the S.O.P., you will also be asked about server training. One way caterers can protect their guests and their clients is to hire only "Smart-Served" staff, who have completed training in responsible drinking. You should have only Smart-Served staff present who will assist your guests to drink responsibly. They will inform the host if they have to "cut off" service to someone who has reached their limit. Often a host will say, "Oh, they're okay, just serve one more." Realize that the servers are present to protect both you as the host and your guests from hurting themselves or others due to intoxication, and the "just one more" could put your guests in danger. They are the sober ones at your party and their judgment is un-impaired. Let them look after you!

Liability is one of the reasons for Smart Service. In recent cases, if an intoxicated guest has been injured or has injured someone else either at a party or after leaving a party, the host/bartender/catering service/restaurant/bar can all share the liability if a lawsuit arises. It has been found in many cases that a bartender who has served to excess is liable for any damages done by the guest following an evening of partying. This is a pretty sobering thought. This explains why caterers at off-premise events are hesitant to take responsibility for your guests.

So once the liability issues have been dealt with:

Caterers do provide bar service, and usually at reasonable rates, offering competitive rates based on consumption, and the service of bringing the alcohol to you, then removing it at the end of the evening, all with a low handling fee. If you have ever supplied alcohol, mixes, garnish, ice, etc. for an event, you know that it's a lot of back-breaking work, as well as the added stress wondering "Have I bought enough?" Caterers provide bar service all the time and are proficient in making sure that they have a sufficient supply. Also, if they find they are running low, they will make a special trip out to supply more liquor, with your permission.

Another issue that can arise is the number of bars you should have set up at your event. Usually, we set up a bar for every 75 to 100 guests, with a bartender ratio of 1 bartender to every 75 guests. What we also suggest is a passed "greeter drink" which will result in shorter queues at the bar and quicker, more efficient service for those who wish an alternate beverage. And please, always make sure you have food around during the event. This is to slow the effects of the liquor on an empty stomach. Caterers want to provide a wonderful service for your event, but as you can see, it is almost a science, as well as a lot of work! But as we do it all the time, we know what needs to be done and look after all the running around so you, the client, can enjoy you party.

When attending a well-planned party, it seems to run flawlessly. Drinks flow, food is served and cleared away, and there never seems to be any mess! Creating a smooth-running affair is not just about colour and imagination—there is a fair bit of science behind a fabulous party! When a caterer asks you a lot of questions before giving you a full estimate, it is because they are trying to determine all the variables in the "Party equation." This way, they can determine the correct ratios and amounts of items needed to send to your event to make your event a success!

Space and Timing

For any event, space is the primary concern. There is no point in having a party if the guests can't move about comfortably, or conversely are lost in a too-large space! When planning a stand-up cocktail reception, have 2.5 square feet per person for comfort, plus ample room for Bars, stationary tables and furniture. For sit-down meals, a 60"round table seating 10 guests each will require a 10-foot square area.

Allow at least an hour for cocktails before your meal to allow guests to arrive, check their coats, have a cocktail and hors d'oeuvres and generally relax and mingle. There is nothing worse than arriving "fashionably late" to a party to find it halfway through! For sit-down meals, with proper staffing, you can estimate at least 30 minutes per course to serve, eat and clear, so a 3-course meal should ostensibly take 1.5 hours from appetizer to coffee service. When planning buffet service, each buffet set-up can serve 75 guests in a 20 to 30 minute time frame.

STAFFING

The staff at an event can make or break your event, without doubt. An understaffed party can quickly deteriorate and create undue stress on the guests, staff and host. Harried staff are unable to provide their best service, and they know it. The following guidelines are used to properly staff an event:

Any party should have an event Supervisor who is responsible for the "whole picture", along with the following:

Bartenders: Minimum one bartender per 60 to 80 guests. With specialty drinks such as blender drinks or Martinis, there should be one bartender per 40 guests.

Cocktail Reception Waiters: Minimum one waiter per 25/40 guests depending on the duration of the event. If you need to serve a lot of food in a short space of time, you should have more staff.

Buffet Dinner Waiters: Minimum one waiter per 25 guests, to effectively set up, serve and clear plates, glassware, etc.

Sit-Down Meal Waiters: Minimum one waiter per 12 guests for good service. If you decrease the ratio, your service level will increase.

Chefs: Your caterer will recommend minimum Chef requirements for your event depending on the complexity of your menu and the kitchen facilities available.

Also, make sure you budget enough time for staff to set-up and tear-down (at least 1.5 hours before the event to set up a cocktail reception and 2 hours for a plated or buffet meal. Allow for a half hour to an hour following the event to tear-down and clean up.

Equipment

Having sufficient equipment at your event is mandatory. Renting the proper amounts of glassware, china and cutlery will ensure a smooth-running event. Do not scrimp on this part of the event. If you do, your service staff will spend much of the event in the kitchen washing when they could be attending to your guests. When ordering glassware, you should have enough for one glass per person per hour of the reception, plus any tableware to be used for dinner.

When planning a buffet dinner always order an extra 50% more china to allow for "second helpings". For a plated meal, order a dozen extra of each course's settings for unexpected guests or breakage. Be sure to always have proper prep tables and garbage receptacles on hand as well as bar wipes for the messes that will always occur! When planning a specialty drink, ensure there is at leas one glass per person as everyone will want to try it!

The Food

It goes without saying that you NEVER want to run out of food. When planning a cocktail party that takes place over the dinner hour, budget for at least 8 pieces of hors d'oeuvres per person. When planning a pre-dinner cocktail event, 3 to 4 pieces of hors d'oeuvres per person will suffice. A sit-down meal can never really run out of food unless a greater number of guests turn up for the event. Buffets are a little trickier to plan, as guests will pick a little bit of each item and not a whole portion, so caterers send partial portions of each item per person. But if there are shrimp items on the buffet, plan for at least 3 pieces per person! Your caterer will ask for the duration of your event to ensure sufficient food quantities.

The Beverages

For some people, the food is the highlight at an event, for others a well-stocked bar will suffice! Planning a fully-stocked bar for a full-evening event (for example, a cocktail reception with a dinner meal) is tricky, but the following guidelines can make it a little simpler: On average, guests will consume 3 to 6 alcoholic beverages per full evening. But that said, as you never really know what your guests will drink, you should have more on hand "just in case." For an all-evening event, you should plan on ordering ½ bottle of wine per person, along with one bottle of beer per person, and one ounce of liquor per person per hour of the event. Should you be serving martinis or specialty cocktails, assume 1.5 ounces per person per hour.

Ensure lots of Mineral water (sparkling and flat), as well as the requisite mixes for the hard liquor you are providing. Bar garnish should always be in abundance as well as ice (4 x 26lb bags per 100 guests, and double it in the summertime!) It is always better to go higher with your liquor purchase, as you can return unopened, undamaged bottles to the LCBO for full credit. Please bear in mind the liquor laws of Ontario stipulating that "An adequate supply of food must be available to persons attending the event. Snacks such as chips, peanuts or popcorn are not an acceptable substitute for this requirement."

Catering Trends

To begin, the client's vision is paramount to any caterer. Usually, we are given certain parameters to work with, and are responsible for executing their plan. Themed parties have always been a trend. So, if we are throwing a 50th Birthday party and the theme is the 1950's, a "Happy Days" party with appropriate food, décor and waiter outfits would be a great choice, and there is no limit to the creativity that can be found in one party, with specialty invitations, custom venue, décor, costuming, etc. The possibilities are endless.

Food

Classic familiar meats with big taste are making a comeback. Grilled Beef Tenderloin with Onion Rings is back as well as Pork Tenderloin. An extremely popular way of presenting these courses is through a tasting menu with many small courses giving a cleaner, leaner look, paired with wines that are course-appropriate. Trendy courses will include seared Tuna, salads with Blue Cheese and candied nuts, as well as Artisanal artistic cCcheese presentations. Multi-grain risottos with sweet potato, barley and quinoa are a big hit, especially with our esteemed vegetarian clients.

Fowl is free-range and vegetables are organic with quality and big flavour the names of the game. Foie Gras is also emerging as a popular item primarily at cocktail parties, due to its restrictive pricing. Near-extinct fish such as Chilean Sea Bass and the over-used Salmon have been replaced with Arctic Char or Halibut and are getting a lot of press. Beginning and rounding off the evening are bite-sized hors d'oeuvres and "mini-mini" desserts, bursting with flavour but not immense in size.

Ethnic foods such as East Indian and Dim Sum are becoming more traditional, moving away from fusion creations and are incorporating themselves quite nicely into trendy-themed "Taste of Toronto" evenings. They are a huge hit with visiting conventions, showcasing the multicultural nature of our city. Also on the rise are mixed-culture weddings that request a blend of two different types of cuisine (i.e. Italian and Indian) which feature elements of both cultures to a spectacular effect. Another trend making its way into our events are foods featuring both local and national Canadian foods, such as Canadian Caviar, Quebec Farm Cheeses, Arctic Char, and gamey meats such as Venison and Bison.

Beverages

The martini just refuses to die, and has reinvented itself with ingredients such as Saki, Champagne, flavoured Vodkas and fresh fruit purées. The mini bottle of Champagne consumed with a straw is still "in" and clients are consuming better wines with their meals. It seems that less is more, which reflects in the beer choices of today, with lighter beers such as Stella Artois, Becks, Heineken, Corona and Sol leading the pack of imports which are a little off the beaten beer track! And don't forget the summer blender drinks, which will never go out of style!

Presentation and Decoration

Presentation is everything. You can have the best tasting food in the world, but if it is not presented with flair, then it loses its appeal. Your entire event hinges on this premise. The trend is now veering sharply towards a clean, lean look. Gone are the days of multiple draped linens, and some events are beginning to be completely linen-free! Seating is at square or rectangular tables made of stainless steel, glass and plexi-glass. High-top tables are interspersed with regular sized dining tables. This "club look" is often accented with sofas, coffee tables and ottomans, giving the event a funky, yet comfortable ambience.

And lighting has also become a major factor in giving events their spark. Intelligent lighting with company logos, snowflakes or changing colours can be combined with laser lights or a simple par light washing the room with an ambient glow. And don't forget your candles, now available in multi-coloured votives or square glass containers. Flowers are less "arranged" and lean toward bunches of similar-coloured cut flowers presented in low glass containers, or single stems in a simple glass.

When linens are used, tablecloths and chair covers are used to transform a room and set a specific tone and are available in a wide array of colours and textures. As for food presentation, courses are routinely presented on square plates, frosted glass, ice containers and unusual bowls. Food stations offering one or two items on tiny plates have replaced sprawling buffets with multiple items and arrays of chafing dishes.

Caterer Can Do

Generally, caterers provide food. This is the simplified version. Actually, most caterers provide food and the immediate services and equipment required to serve this food. But increasingly, caterers are becoming more "event-savvy", and are providing a wider array of services. How can you maximize your caterer's services? What can a caterer do for me?

Venue Search

The most overlcoked service that your caterer can provide is the one that can launch your event: The search for a venue. If you are looking for that "perfect place", your caterer will be able to find the ideal venue for you. Most caterers are intimately familiar with Toronto's best venues, and they can quickly suggest the one that will match your taste, requirements and budget. This translates to huge time savings, and best of all—It's free!

Rentals and Décor

On top of the standard table, chair and glassware rental, most caterers are also knowledgeable about other decorative rental items. Although the rental industry has matured over the past ten years, offering both great selection and huge inventories, a growing number of specialized companies have surfaced (i.e. linens, specialty bars, china, candles, etc.) The skills and strengths of a good caterer is to know about everything available and to suggest the best available selection from the many diverse suppliers.

Caterers know where to go to source specialty items, and can, with a little finesse, turn a reception into a Special Event! Also, ordering rental equipment is an art in itself, as the right number of each item can ensure a seamless event. On site, the caterer will also take responsibility, so you are not running around at the last minute worrying about details! Specialty décor items such as lighting, flowers, props and furniture are also a no-brainer, as your caterer will know what needs highlighting and how much space you have to work with. You can leave all the worries to them and enjoy your event!

Staffing

Your caterer will hire professional staff for your event. The quality and caliber of service provided today has greatly improved over the past few years, and the sign of a good caterer is their ability to match the best staff with the intricacies of the event, and to book sufficient staff for the event. By allowing your caterer to provide this service, they will take responsibility if there is an unforeseen issue (i.e. staff does not show up due to illness). They are acutely aware of the strengths of the people they employ, and, as the service staff works frequently with the caterer, they are mindful of the caterer's food, set-up, service and take-down expectations.

Help from well-meaning volunteers and/or children is also an issue that often arises, and while the idea is admirable, it does not often work out in the best interests of your event. Caterers are understandably reluctant to become involved with such assistance due to a lack of experience and also increasingly strict liability issues.

Event Co-Ordination

One of the most common pitfalls at events is how the control of the event is managed. As the client, you have done an amazing job at selecting the very best suppliers and sharing your visions with them. However, on the day of the event, many questions arise as the many unfamiliar (with each other) suppliers arrive to set up their work, and their creations. Event set-up can be likened to an orchestra where the conductor is the client and the musicians are the suppliers. When the client is unavailable to answer questions or is socializing with their guests, the chaos begins and the orchestra loses its direction. The result is a less-than-perfect symphony!

All the good will and research at gathering the best suppliers is wasted as there is no supervision at this critical time during set-up, and often the outcome is a less-than-perfect event. There are two ways in which to avoid potential disaster: The easiest way is to allow the caterer to subcontract the "players" in your event from the outset. This way, there is a clear line of control, eliminating the opportunity for chaos, or; If you choose to hire your own suppliers, consider hiring an Event Planner who will supervise and coordinate the details on your behalf. The result will be a smooth-running event that mirrors your original vision.

In closing, the goal of hiring a caterer is to "Be a Guest at your own Party" so allowing them to do what they do best, you can sit back, relax and enjoy the event, your guests and the whole experience. Let the caterer handle all the details, while you accept the compliments of your happy guests!

How To Choose A Caterer

Most people have never thought of entertaining on a grand scale, and the thought of providing food, alcohol, entertainment, etc. for a large number of people can be daunting for the uninitiated! When throwing a party, it should reflect your tastes, personality and sense of adventure, and selecting the appropriate caterer can make the entire process effortless. Tales of nightmarish events are plentiful, and you don't want to be remembered as one of them! However, do not fear.

The catering industry in Toronto rivals those in other large U.S. cities and the services we offer are world class. But how do you decide which caterer is best for you? When polled, event professionals agree: word of mouth is the best way in which to find your caterer of choice. When doing your initial fact-finding, ask friends or business associates whom they have used in the past. Large companies often have an in-house event planner who will be in the know. Ask your florist, DJ, or rental company for recommendations.

Industry professionals tend to associate only with organizations who excel at what they do. Also, venues in your area are a great source of information. Call them and ask for their lists of approved caterers. You can be sure that venue-approved caterers have been qualified and meet the high standards of the venue. When attending events, ask questions: Who is catering the event? How is the food? Are the service staff friendly and polite? Did you have to wait for service?

Moreover, bend the ear of your host/ess and inquire about the caterer's service during the planning process: Was the planning enjoyable? Was the consultant enthusiastic? Remember, the experience of a party is not simply how it appears at the actual event, the planning process should be enjoyable as well. Web-sites allow you to get a quick introduction and feel for the company, but be aware that the skills of the web-designer may actually enhance or mask the company's actual abilities. Finally, consistency is one of the cornerstones for your selection as it is your assurance that you will get the best service time after time!

The purpose of all this preliminary research is to narrow the field to those caterers you wish to interview for your event. Decide on a select few who seem to fit your needs. Asking for too many estimates creates an avalanche of unnecessary work for yourself!

Caterer Styles

Understanding your caterer's area of specialty and his limits is paramount to ensuring a successful event. Caterer expertise can be divided into the following three categories:

Luncheon Caterer: Providing good, simple food, with a limited selection of cuisine.

Gourmet Caterer: Increased knowledge of food , more creative, able to provide cocktail, sit-down and buffet meals, somewhat limited in coordinating and providing related services such as consultations, rental equipment, wait-staff, etc

Full service event caterer: Specialize in a vast array of foods and services, coordination, décor and can handle large number of patrons with ease. By selecting the caterer in the right category for your event, you will ensure yourself a higher chance of success.

Once you have decided upon the caterers you wish to interview, you should assemble some information: First, you should be able to communicate to your potential caterers your goals for the party. Are you celebrating a special occasion in a warm, intimate style? Do you want a funky, fun atmosphere? Are there important clients you would like to impress? Second, have some sort of a budget in mind before approaching your caterer. This is not easy to do, but developing a range is paramount.

The cost of a reception varies wildly by caterer and type of event, but ultimately it is the size of the party, venue choice, type of food and service that will determine the price. Your catering consultant will discuss your budget with you and let you know if your expectations are realistic. A good caterer will make your money work for you. Third, be ready to answer some specific questions related to your proposed event. Your caterer will need some details so they can prepare an accurate estimate for you. Make sure that all potential caterers are given the same information so that you can compare equally.

Questions they may ask you will include: What is the venue for your event? Is it an elegant black-tie affair or a fun filled birthday celebration? Is there equipment available for the caterer use at the venue (i.e. tables, chairs, kitchen amenities)? Will you require a tent? What kind of bar do you wish to have? Are there any guests with specific needs, allergies, or tastes? All these will affect your budget. Most caterers will (and should) provide you with a detailed estimate, which will outline the breakdown of services and clearly state the costs that can fluctuate. Once you have the estimates, you can determine which organization has understood your ideas for your event.

Keep in mind, though, that catering is a very seasonal business. During certain months, caterers are extremely busy working on events. Caterers do their utmost to provide the best service and they require ample notice to develop a custom proposal with your unique needs. Frequently, they have to gather information and estimates from other suppliers in order to give you an accurate estimate. For obvious reasons, December is every caterer's busiest month and while we have good intentions of getting you the information you require with speed and accuracy, a little patience goes a long way...

Your Consultant

Your entire experience should be a positive one, beginning with the first contact with your catering consultant. Are your ideas received with enthusiasm? Are they asking relevant questions? Do they provide alternative suggestions and ideas? Are they excited about your event? A lot of your time will be spent with your consultant, and you should feel at ease and most importantly, listened to for your ideas to be properly interpreted and to ensure a successful event. A consultant worth his or her salt will have a personal stake in the success of your event. You should have full confidence in their abilities.

The Interview

At this stage of the game, you have probably gathered estimates from your chosen caterers. The next step is to meet with your consultant to get an up close and personal feel about their services. From the estimates, you will be better equipped to ask detailed questions. Don't be shy about asking for client references and request photos, if they have them. Is your consultant confident, personable and enthuastic about planning your party? Your meeting with them should be a positive one, if you leave feeling doubts or apprehension about the caterer, then keep looking.

The Tasting

Caterers have mixed feelings about tastings. Some offer them, and some do not. It is widely held, though, that a tasting is offered only once your party is booked and you wish to taste the menu that you have confirmed with your consultant. The tasting is more of a finalizing of the event, not a sales point as it is very expensive to produce, as well as time-consuming. It is not meant as an "evening out", so please do not invite your family, friends, co-workers, etc. You should keep your decision-making team to a minimum, or it turns into a catered party that will be charged accordingly.

Once you have met with the various caterers, you can make a confident decision about who will be best able to cater for you. Remember that catering is an art. Going to unknown venues, working in ill-equipped kitchens, being creative, dealing with weather conditions, etc., all of these factors requires good organization, skill and talent. Toss in time and budget restraints... this will demand someone who has experience and knowledge, as well as a love of food and parties!

Once you have chosen your caterer, listen to their ideas. They have done this before and can offer beneficial advice on creating a successful party. They are professionals who take the "Art of Partying" seriously. Finally, execution of a catered event does not rest solely upon the quality of the food served. It is the successful fusion of planning, service and food.

10

Marketing of Flavoured Alcoholic Beverages

Flavoured alcoholic beverages (FABs) were first introduced into the alcohol market in the early 1980s in the form of wine coolers. FABs are sweet, relatively low alcohol content beverages that are designed for "entry-level" drinkers. The alcohol industry has introduced new products and production methods to expand the category's popularity.

Wine coolers, the first entry into the "Flavoured alcoholic beverages" were introduced into the United States by two young entrepreneurs in 1980. The new beverage had an instant success. Gallo and Seagrams, two large producers, used their distribution and marketing muscle to dominate the new market. By the early 1990s, wine coolers' popularity had plateaued, and many considered the product line a fad.

A second phase of the FAB category emerged in the mid 1990s from Australia and Great Britain in the form of "alcopops", a lemonflavoured concoction that could have a malt, wine, or distilled spirit base. Alcopops migrated to the United States in 1996, and major producers began to market them internationally. As with wine coolers, the large producers stepped into the market after the success of the small producers, bringing their marketing networks and resources to expand sales and global availability.

By the late 1990s, the distilled spirits industry stepped into the alcopops market, creating a third wave of beverages which they labeled "Flavoured malt beverages" (FMBs). FMBs carry distilled spirits brand names, such as Bacardi Silver, Smirnoff Ice, and Skyy Blue, but, as with most coolers and alcopops, have relatively low alcohol content. The labels and marketing are controlled by distillers, who contract the production to beer producers.

Distillers had been frustrated by the aging of their primary consumer base and the erosion of their market among younger drinkers, who prefer beer and other low alcohol products. Introducing drinkers to spirits-branded FMBs creates brand awareness for spirits. The introduction of FMBs triggered a renewed surge in the FAB market. Between 1998 to 2003, global FAB sales increased 161% in volume.

In the United States, the market more than doubled between 1998 and 2002. Switzerland's imports of FABs went up from two million bottles to 39 million between 2000 and 2002. Smirnoff Ice and Bacardi Breezer became the two most popular brands, with 11.4% and 4.7% share of the global market in 2002, respectively. Despite declining sales in some countries, regional market sales forecasts for FABs predict continued worldwide growth.

Sales in the United States and several other developed countries dominate the FAB market, but future expansion is expected to occur in other parts of the globe. Euromonitor International, a leading provider of global alcohol market intelligence, predicts that particularly rapid volume growth in the Eastern European region between 2003 and 2008 (63.9%).

Other global regional markets with expected significant growth during this time frame are: Australasia

(48.3%), Western Europe (46.4%), Asia Pacific (42.3%), and Latin America (22.5%). Even the Africa/Middle East region, a tiny portion of the FAB global market (dominated by South Africa), can expect a significant 26% increase. By contrast, Euromonitor predicts only a 6.9% growth rate for the North American region. These market predictions suggest FAB producers plan to use FABs as an integral part of its broader strategy for globalising the alcohol market.

Youth and Flavoured Alcoholic Beverages (FABs)

FABs are popular with underage drinkers, including very young teenagers. Youth wine cooler consumption was conducted in the United States in 1991 by the Inspector General for the US Department of Health and Human Services. Junior and senior high school students drank 35% of all wine coolers sold in the United States; and Wine coolers were the favourite alcoholic beverage among 42.1% of students who drink.

Sweden found that the introduction of alcopops accounted for approximately half of the increase in alcohol consumption by 15-to-16-years-old boys from 1996 to 1999, and two-thirds of the increase among girls. This was a period in Sweden when alcohol consumption among adults had stabilised but youth consumption increased. A 1999 Welsh survey reported that 17% of youth 11-to-16-years-old consumed alcopops at least once a week, a substantial percentage of this age group did not drink other types of alcoholic beverages, and the increase in youth consumption in the previous year matched the consumption rates of the youth drinking exclusively alcopops.

According to a recent news analysis, a German government report in 2003 estimated that 50% of alcopops are purchased by 14-to-19-years-old. Youth FABs consumption patterns between 1996 and 2003. In 2003, the latest data available, 20% of 12-to-13-years-old and 41% of 14-to-15-years-old consumed FABs in the previous week. In both age groups, girls reported drinking more FABs than boys. The distillers' strategy of using FABs to cut into the youth beer market is succeeding

Between 1996 and 2003, consumption of beer and wine drunk by 14-to-15-years-old in the United Kingdom declined substantially, resulting in larger market shares for alcopops and spirits. FABs among young teenagers, particularly girls, and suggest that FAB youth consumption is associated with serious public health harm.

The American Medical Association (AMA) in 2004 found that approximately one-third of teenaged girls and one-fifth of teenaged boys have tried alcopops. Thirty-four percent of teenagers in the survey incorrectly thought that alcopops have less alcohol than beer or similar drinks. Of teen girls who have tried FABs: one-fifth have "thrown up or passed out from drinking", one-fourth have "driven after drinking or ridden in a car with a driver who had been drinking", and one-sixth have been "sexually active after drinking".

Girls in particular are attracted to FABs, reporting higher rates of 30-day prevalence for these products than beer. For boys, the consumption of the two products is similar in the eighth grade, but beer becomes more popular with age. About one-third of all high school seniors report regular consumption of FABs. These figures are remarkable, since beer has 33 times the volume sales of FABs, indicating that a large percentage of the FAB market is consumed by underage drinkers.

Unfortunately, youth consumption data are not available from other parts of the world. However, these studies, conducted mostly in countries with relatively high volumes of FAB sales, suggest that as the FABs become a global commodity, they are likely to be particularly popular in the youth market. Despite the mounting evidence of disproportionate youth FAB consumption, FAB producers continue to maintain that their products are designed for and consumed by adults and that their marketing does not target underage drinkers.

MARKETING STRATEGIES

According to the US Federal Trade Commission (FTC), "adults 21 to 29 appear to be the intended target of [FAB] marketing", and there is no evidence that underage drinkers are a significant portion of the FAB market. The FTC reached this conclusion even though the report acknowledges that FAB advertising reaches a "substantial youth audience" and some themes in the advertising and the sweet taste of the beverages "may also be attractive to minors". The Commission refused to consider any epidemiological or marketing evidence other than documents supplied by the industry and did not conduct an independent investigation. The industry did not supply the FTC with any data regarding youth consumption.

The FTC's limited investigation notwithstanding, there is considerable evidence that FAB marketing does in fact target underage drinkers. Marketing strategies can be analysed using the four "P's" of marketing. product, promotion, place, and price. Marketers coordinate these four key elements to develop a "total marketing" programme to reach target audiences and consumers.

Product

The product variable focuses on the development of the product itself, including its ingredients, taste, colour, alcohol content, and packaging. FABs' sweet taste and fruity flavours are specifically designed to bridge the taste of soft drinks and traditional alcoholic beverages, providing a pathway for those not accustomed to the harsher tastes of distilled spirits, beer and wine.

Industry representatives do not deny this fundamental purpose of the FAB category: FABs are designed to reach "new drinkers" or "entry-level drinkers" or some similar term. Euromonitor International's report TheWorld Market for Spirits and FABs, states: "No matter where in the world they are drunk, and at what kind of occasion, there is no doubt that FABs are consumed by younger drinkers. The combination of packaging, taste and alcoholic content gives them little appeal to older drinkersy".

The industry counters arguments that FABs are therefore designed for young teenagers by claiming that the "new drinkers" that are being targeted are over the legal drinking age. This is clearly not the case. In the United States, for example, research demonstrates most drinkers begin consumption well before they are 21, the US minimum drinking age. The age of initiation has been dropping steadily in the last four decades in the United states, from 17.6 years in 1965 to 15.9 years in 1999. For 12-to-20-years-old only, the average age of first use in 2000 was only 14 years old.

Only 15.5% of young people had not used alcohol by their twentieth birthday. In other words "new drinkers" who might be attracted to "a bridge" to traditional alcoholic beverages are almost all under 21 years of age. Introducing FABs into the market provides a vehicle for promoting the continuing decline in the age of initiation. Although many countries have lower minimum drinking ages, beverages that target new drinkers with unsophisticated tastes are still young teenagers not old enough to legally consume alcohol.

The Center for Science in the Public Interest (CSPI) in the United States among 600 teenagers aged 14-to-18 years and among 500 adults provide further evidence of youth targeting in the FAB product design. Nearly nine of ten teenagers in the surveys cited taste as an important factor in consuming FABs. Large majorities of both youth and adult respondents believe that FAB producers use sweet flavour that masks the harsher tastes of beer and distilled spirits precisely to make them appealing to young people. Most teenagers believe the products are being marketed to people their own age or younger.

Promotion

The promotion element of total marketing involves the marketing message and its placement in the media. "Measured media" includes television, radio, print, and outdoor advertising. "Unmeasured media" refers to non-traditional forms of media such as the Internet, product placement (e.g., in movies), and sponsorship of sporting events and concerts. Like other alcohol marketers, FAB producers are increasingly relying on unmeasured media to communicate its marketing messages.

The surges in FAB sales documented above occur concurrently with equally impressive increases in spending on promotions. FAB producers in the United States, for example, increased their spending in measured media from $27.5 million in 2000 to $196.3 million in 2002, a seven-fold increase, the same period that sales increased by 52%. Spending on unmeasured media was probably two to three times this amount, suggesting that total FAB promotions' spending in the United States in 2002 was $600 million or more.

On the Internet, FAB producers during 2003 maintained websites that contained interactive games, chat rooms, downloadable wallpaper and screensavers, videos, merchandise, and other materials highly attractive to youth. Underage youth account for tens of thousands of visits to these sites each year, and the producers fail to take even minimal steps to reduce youth exposure.

The AMA survey found that adult women were far less likely than teenage girls to report that they had seen or heard FAB advertisements on television, radio, the Internet, or in stores. Similarly, the surveys conducted in the United States by the Global Strategy Group found that teenagers (6%) are greater than three times more likely than adults (21%) to have seen, heard or read about FABs, and young teenagers (14-16 years of age - 62%) have only slightly lower awareness than older teenagers (17-18 years of age - 65%).

Placement/Availability

The placement component of total marketing addresses where the product is available for purchase and consumption. A high priority for FAB producers is having their products widely available, particularly in sales outlets where young people are likely to be present, such as neighborhood convenience stores, grocery stores, and gas stations.

Large producers are able to dominate the FAB market because of their extensive distribution networks. In many countries, a key to expanding availability is having FABs be classified as beer rather than wine or distilled spirits. Throughout the United States, for example, there are three times as many beer retail off-premises outlets as spirits retail off-premises outlets.

State and local laws vary widely, but in general, beer outlets (such as convenience and grocery stores) are more likely to be frequented by young people. A recent World Health Organisation (WHO) report found that these differences in beer and distilled spirits availability are common in other parts of the world.

Price

The fourth component of total marketing - price - is of critical importance to marketing products to young people, who are price sensitive and therefore less likely to consume alcohol as prices increase. As with availability, classifying FABs as beer can result in lower prices because in most countries beer is taxed at lower rates than either distilled spirits or wine. In the United States, for example, distilled spirits taxes can be five to ten times higher by volume than beer taxes.

One industry commentator attributed the decline in wine coolers in the United States (and increase in malt-based FABs) directly to federal increases in the wine tax. The WHO found in its global report on alcohol that similar differences in tax rates between distilled spirits and beer in most of the 60 countries where data was available.

Distilled Spirit

Most national governments and their governmental subdivisions do not treat FABs as a separate beverage category for tax and regulatory purposes. As a result, governments must determine for each specific brand of FAB whether it should be classified as beer, wine or distilled spirit. Definitions vary, but in most cases the legal definitions rely on the origin of the alcohol in the product. The appropriate governmental inquiry for determining how to classify FABs, then, is to determine whether the alcohol was brewed from malt, grapes (beer or wine) or distilled.

FAB producers in many countries seek a beer classification because of the advantages associated with tax rates and availability regulations. This creates a dilemma for FAB producers, because using alcohol brewed from malt in FABs creates an unpleasant taste that is difficult and expensive to mask.

FAB producers in the United States developed an innovative solution to the problem. FABs may have beer as a part of the base beverage, but the alcohol, taste, and colour of the beer are removed, and other liquids and flavours are added. The alcohol in the final product is derived primarily from the additives, which contain distilled alcohol and has little or no resemblance to the original beer used as the base beverage.

The US Alcohol and Tobacco Trade and Tax Bureau (TTB), 83% of the 114 FABs tested contained less than 25% of the original beer and, for 92% of the brands tested, 75% or more of the alcohol derived from added distilled alcohol. The producers use this peculiar process in order to claim that the final product should be classified as beer for regulatory and tax purposes. Since the regulatory advantages of the beer classification do not occur in all countries, differing production processes are used depending on the regulatory climate.

Diageo's Smirnoff Ice has a different formulation in the United States than in other countries where it is identified as a spirits-based beverage. The alcopops brand Hooch has a malt base in the United States, a spirit base in the United Kingdom and a fruit wine base in Germany. The producers' strategy, however, has a major flaw. Most legal definitions of beer and distilled spirits are not based on what beverage is used as a base but rather on the type of alcohol in the final product. FABs that contain a high percentage of distilled alcohol (derived from additives) should be treated as distilled spirits, not beer.

FABs should be classified as distilled spirits by the federal government and most states, a fact that FAB producers were aware since at least 1996. Yet the producers continued to represent their products as beer to regulators, resulting in lower taxes and greater availability and advertising outlets. Even the label given to the products ("Flavoured Malt Beverages" or "malternatives") promoted the legal misclassification.

The federal and state governmental response to the distillers' deceptive FAB marketing practices in the United States provides a case study of how industries can dominate the agencies that are supposed to regulate them. The Bureau of Alcohol, Tobacco and Firearms (BATF), the original federal agency with jurisdiction over FABs, held in March 1996 that, under federal law, FABs that contained distilled alcohol from additives should be classified as distilled spirits and not beer.

Yet the ruling had an unprecedented component: It stated that the agency would not enforce the law pending the development of new regulations. In the interim, BATF stated that producers could violate the law and continue to treat FABs as beer provided the products contained less than 6% alcohol by volume.

The promised rule making, which was to occur in the "near future", took nearly 9 years, during which FAB sales surged. In March 2003, the Trade and Tax Bureau (TTB), the successor bureau to BATF, issued a notice of rule change. It proposed classifying FMBs which contain more than 0.5% added distilled product as distilled spirits. Two years later, in January 2005, TTB made a final decision, which responded to the intensive political lobbying campaign by distillers and FAB producers.

TTB decided against the proposed 0.5% distilled spirits rule, instead ruling that up to 49% of the alcohol in FABs could be derived from distilled alcohol. The Bureau also gave the industry one year to comply. The decision was justified based on a finding that the 0.5%

proposed rule would cause undue economic hardship to small producers of FMBs (even though the market is dominated by large producers). Potential public health impacts of the regulatory decision were not addressed, nor did the Bureau analyse the apparent conflict between its decision and BATF's interpretation of the underlying federal law.

In the United States, the states have independent authority to classify alcohol products, and most states have definitions that would classify FABs as distilled spirits instead of beer. Nevertheless, the FAB producers convinced state regulators in every state but Oregon to delay any regulatory action until the federal government issued its own rules. With the January 2005 ruling, states can expect an intensive lobbying campaign by FAB producers to amend state laws to conform to the federal ruling.

The experience in the United States provides a caution for other countries seeking to limit underage consumption of FABs. The producers will alter production techniques to gain regulatory and tax advantages even though the final product is identical across geographical borders. In the United States, for example, the misclassification of FABs as beer instead of distilled spirits has resulted in substantial losses in state revenues, estimated in one study to be at least $260.6 million in 2002 alone.

11

Staff Management

Food and beverage serving and related workers are the front line of customer service in restaurants, coffee shops, and other food service establishments. These workers greet customers, escort them to seats and hand them menus, take food and drink orders, and serve food and beverages. They also answer questions, explain menu items and specials, and keep tables and dining areas clean and set for new diners. Most work as part of a team, helping coworkers during busy times to improve workflow and customer service.

Waiters and waitresses, the largest group of these workers, take customers' orders, serve food and beverages, prepare itemised checks, and sometimes accept payment. Their specific duties vary considerably, depending on the establishment. In coffee shops serving routine, straightforward fare, such as salads, soups, and sandwiches, servers are expected to provide fast, efficient, and courteous service.

In fine dining restaurants, where more complicated meals are prepared and often served over several courses, waiters and waitresses provide more formal service emphasising personal, attentive treatment and a more leisurely pace. They may recommend certain dishes and identify ingredients or explain how various items on the menu are prepared. Some prepare salads, desserts, or other menu items tableside. Additionally, they may check the identification of patrons to ensure they meet the minimum age requirement for the purchase of alcohol and tobacco products.

Waiters and waitresses sometimes perform the duties of other food and beverage service workers. These tasks may include escorting guests to tables, serving customers seated at counters, clearing and setting up tables, or operating a cash register. However, full-service restaurants frequently hire other staff, such as hosts and hostesses, cashiers, or dining room attendants, to perform these duties.

Bartenders fill drink orders either taken directly from patrons at the bar or through waiters and waitresses who place drink orders for dining room customers. Bartenders check identification of customers seated at the bar, to ensure they meet the minimum age requirement for the purchase of alcohol and tobacco products. They prepare mixed drinks, serve bottled or draught beer, and pour wine or other beverages.

Bartenders must know a wide range of drink recipes and be able to mix drinks accurately, quickly, and without waste. Besides mixing and serving drinks, bartenders stock and prepare garnishes for drinks; maintain an adequate supply of ice, glasses, and other bar supplies; and keep the bar area clean for customers. They also may collect payment, operate the cash register, wash glassware and utensils, and serve food to customers seated at the bar. Bartenders usually are responsible for ordering and maintaining an inventory of liquor, mixes, and other bar supplies.

The majority of bartenders directly serve and interact with patrons. Bartenders should be friendly and enjoy mingling with customers. Bartenders at service bars, on the other hand, have less contact with customers. They work in small bars often located off the kitchen in restaurants, hotels, and clubs where only waiters and waitresses place drink orders. Some establishments, especially larger, higher volume ones, use equipment that automatically pours and mixes drinks at the push of a button. Bartenders who use this equipment, however, still must work quickly to handle a large volume of drink orders and be familiar with the ingredients for special drink requests. Much of a bartender's work still must be done by hand to fill each individual order.

Hosts and hostesses welcome guests and maintain reservation or waiting lists. They may direct patrons to coatrooms, restrooms, or to a place to wait until their table is ready. Hosts and hostesses assign guests to tables suitable for the size of their group, escort patrons to their seats, and provide menus. They also schedule dining reservations, arrange parties, and organise any special services that are required. In some restaurants, they act as cashiers.

Dining room and cafeteria attendants and bartender helpers assist waiters, waitresses, and bartenders by cleaning tables, removing dirty dishes, and keeping serving areas stocked with supplies. Sometimes called backwaiters or runners, they bring meals out of the kitchen and assist waiters and waitresses by distributing dishes to individual diners. They also replenish the supply of clean linens, dishes, silverware, and glasses in the dining room and keep the bar stocked with glasses, liquor, ice, and drink garnishes.

Dining room attendants set tables with clean tablecloths, napkins, silverware, glasses, and dishes and serve ice water, rolls, and butter. At the conclusion of meals, they remove dirty dishes and soiled linens from tables. Cafeteria attendants stock serving tables with food, trays, dishes, and silverware and may carry trays to dining tables for patrons. Bartender helpers keep bar equipment clean and wash glasses. Dishwashers clean dishes, cutlery, and kitchen utensils and equipment.

Counter attendants take orders and serve food in cafeterias, coffee shops, and carryout eateries. In cafeterias, they serve food displayed on steam tables, carve meat, dish out vegetables, ladle sauces and soups, and fill beverage glasses. In lunchrooms and coffee shops, counter attendants take orders from customers seated at the counter, transmit orders to the kitchen, and pick up and serve food. They also fill cups with coffee, soda, and other beverages and prepare fountain specialties, such as milkshakes and ice cream sundaes. Counter attendants also take carryout orders from diners and wrap or place items in containers. They clean counters, write itemised checks, and sometimes accept payment. Some counter attendants may prepare short-order items, such as sandwiches and salads.

Some food and beverage serving workers take orders from customers at counters or drive-through windows at fast-food restaurants. They assemble orders, hand them to customers, and accept payment. Many of these are *combined food preparation and serving workers* who also cook and package food, make coffee, and fill beverage cups using drink-dispensing machines. Other workers serve food to patrons outside of a restaurant environment, such as in hotels, hospital rooms, or cars.

Working Situations

Food and beverage service workers are on their feet most of the time and often carry heavy trays of food, dishes, and glassware. During busy dining periods, they are under pressure to serve customers quickly and efficiently. The work is relatively safe, but care must be taken to avoid slips, falls, and burns.

Part-time work is more common among food and beverage serving and related workers than among workers in almost any other occupation. In 2002, those on part-time schedules included half of all waiters and waitresses, and 2 out of 5 bartenders. Food service and drinking establishments typically maintain long dining hours and offer flexible and varied work opportunities. Many food and beverage serving and related workers work evenings, weekends, and holidays.

Some work split shifts—they work for several hours during the middle of the day, take a few hours off in the afternoon, and then return to their jobs for evening hours. Many students and teenagers seek part time or seasonal work as food and beverage serving and related workers as a first job to gain work experience or to earn spending money while in school. Around one-fourth of food and beverage serving and related workers were 16 to 19 years old—about 5 times the proportion for all workers.

Food and beverage serving and related workers held 6.5 million jobs in 2002. The distribution of jobs among the various food and beverage serving workers was as follows:

Waiters and waitresses	2,097,000
Combined food preparation and serving workers, including fast food	1,990,000
Dishwashers	505,000
Counter attendants, cafeteria, food concession, and coffee	467,000
Bartenders	463,000
Dining room and cafeteria attendants and bartender helpers	409,000
Hosts and hostesses, restaurant, lounge, and coffee shop	298,000
Food servers, nonrestaurant	195,000
All other food preparation and serving related workers	117,000

The overwhelming majority of jobs for food and beverage serving and related workers were found in food services and drinking places, such as restaurants, coffee shops, and bars. Other jobs were found primarily in traveler accommodation (hotels); amusement, gambling, and recreation industries; educational services; grocery stores; nursing care facilities; civic and social organizations; and hospitals.

Jobs are located throughout the country but are typically plentiful in large cities and tourist areas. Vacation resorts offer seasonal employment, and some workers alternate between summer and winter resorts, instead of remaining in one area the entire year.

Training

There are no specific educational requirements for food and beverage service jobs. Many employers prefer to hire high school graduates for waiter and waitress, bartender, and host and hostess positions, but completion of high school usually is not required for fast-food workers, counter attendants, dishwashers, and dining room attendants and bartender helpers. A job as a food and beverage service worker serves as a source of immediate income, rather than a career, for many people. Many entrants to these jobs are in their late teens or early twenties and have a high school education or less. Usually, they have little or no work experience. Many are full-time students or homemakers. Food and beverage service jobs are a major source of part-time employment for high school and college students.

Restaurants rely on good food and quality customer service to retain loyal customers and succeed in a competitive industry. Food and beverage serving and related workers who exhibit excellent personal qualities, such as a neat clean appearance, a well-spoken manner, an ability to work as a member of team, and a pleasant way with patrons, will be highly sought after.

Waiters and waitresses need a good memory to avoid confusing customers' orders and to recall faces, names, and preferences of frequent patrons. These workers also should be comfortable using computers to place orders and generate customers' bills. Some may need to be quick at arithmetic so they can total bills manually. Knowledge of a foreign language is helpful to communicate with a diverse clientele and staff. Prior experience waiting on tables is preferred by restaurants and hotels that have rigid table service standards. Jobs at these establishments often offer higher wages and have greater income potential from tips, but they may also have stiffer employment requirements, such as higher education or training standards, than other establishments.

Usually, bartenders must be at least 21 years of age, but employers prefer to hire people who are 25 or older. Bartenders should be familiar with State and local laws concerning the sale of alcoholic beverages. Most food and beverage serving and related workers pick up their skills on the job by observing and working with more experienced workers. Some employers, particularly those in fast-food restaurants, use self-instruction programmes with audiovisual presentations and instructional booklets to teach new employees food preparation and service skills.

Some public and private vocational schools, restaurant associations, and large restaurant chains provide classroom training in a generalised food service curriculum. Some bartenders acquire their skills by attending a bartending or vocational and technical school. These programmes often include instruction on State and local laws and regulations, cocktail recipes, attire and conduct, and stocking a bar. Some of these schools help their graduates find jobs. Although few employers require any minimum level of educational attainment, some specialised training is usually needed in food handling and legal issues surrounding serving alcoholic beverages and tobacco. Employers are more likely to hire and promote based on people skills and personal qualities rather than education.

Due to the relatively small size of most food-serving establishments, opportunities for promotion are limited. After gaining experience, some dining room and cafeteria attendants and bartender helpers advance to waiter, waitress, or bartender jobs. For waiters, waitresses, and bartenders, advancement usually is limited to finding a job in a busier or more expensive restaurant or bar where prospects for tip earnings are better. A few bartenders open their own businesses. Some hosts and hostesses and waiters and waitresses advance to supervisory jobs, such as maitre d'hotel, dining room supervisor, or restaurant manager. In larger restaurant chains, food and beverage service workers who excel at their work often are invited to enter the company's formal management training programme.

Job Opportunities

Job openings are expected to be abundant for food and beverage serving and related workers. Overall employment of these workers is expected to grow about as fast as the average over the 2002-12 period, stemming from increases in population, personal incomes, and leisure time. While employment growth will account for many new jobs, the overwhelming majority of openings will arise from the need to replace the high proportion of workers who leave the occupations each year.

There is substantial movement into and out of these occupations because education and training requirements are minimal, and the predominance of part-time jobs is attractive to people seeking a short-term source of income rather than a career. However, keen competition is expected for bartender, waiter and waitress, and other food and beverage service jobs in popular restaurants and fine dining establishments, where potential earnings from tips are greatest.

Projected employment growth between 2002 and 2012 varies by type of job. Employment of combined food preparation and serving workers, which includes fast-food workers, is expected to increase faster than the average in response to the continuing fast-paced lifestyle of many Americans and the addition of healthier foods at many fast-food restaurants. Increases in the number of families and the more affluent, 55-and-older population will result in more restaurants that offer table service and more varied menus—leading to average growth for waiters and waitresses and hosts and hostesses.

Employment of dining room attendants and dishwashers will grow more slowly than other food and beverage serving and related workers, because diners increasingly are eating at more casual dining spots, such as coffee bars and sandwich shops, rather than at the full-service restaurants that employ more of these workers. Slower than average employment growth is expected for bartenders.

Wages

Food and beverage serving and related workers derive their earnings from a combination of hourly wages and customer tips. Earnings vary greatly, depending on the type of job and establishment. For example, fast-food workers and hosts and hostesses usually do not receive tips, so their wage rates may be higher than those of waiters and waitresses and bartenders in full-service restaurants, who typically earn more from tips than from wages. In some restaurants, workers contribute a portion of their tips to a tip pool, which is distributed among qualifying workers. Tip pools allow workers who don't usually receive tips directly from customers, such as dining room attendants, to share in the rewards of good service.

In 2002, median hourly earnings (including tips) of waiters and waitresses were $6.80. The middle 50 percent earned between $6.13 and $8.00. The lowest 10 percent earned less than $5.70, and the highest 10 percent earned more than $11.00 an hour. For most waiters and waitresses, higher earnings are primarily the result of receiving more in tips rather than higher hourly wages. Tips usually average between 10 and 20 percent of guests' checks; waiters and waitresses working in busy, expensive restaurants earn the most.

Bartenders had median hourly earnings (including tips) of $7.21 in 2002. The middle 50 percent earned between $6.33 and $9.02. The lowest 10 percent earned less than $5.76, and the highest 10 percent earned more than $11.96 an hour. Like waiters and waitresses, bartenders employed in public bars may receive more than half of their earnings as tips. Service bartenders often are paid higher hourly wages to offset their lower tip earnings.

Median hourly earnings (including tips) of dining room and cafeteria attendants and bartender helpers were $6.99 in 2002. The middle 50 percent earned between $6.33 and $8.10. The lowest 10 percent earned less than $5.80, and the highest 10 percent earned more than $9.70 an hour. Most received over half of their earnings as wages; the rest of their income was a share of the proceeds from tip pools.

Median hourly earnings of hosts and hostesses were $7.36 in 2002. The middle 50 percent earned between $6.54 and $8.58. The lowest 10 percent earned less than $5.89, and the highest 10 percent earned more than $10.32 an hour. Wages comprised the majority of their earnings. In some cases, wages were supplemented by proceeds from tip pools.

Median hourly earnings of combined food preparation and serving workers, including fast food, were $6.97 in 2002. The middle 50 percent earned between $6.23 and $8.08. The lowest 10 percent earned less than $5.74, and the highest 10 percent earned more than $9.33 an hour. Although some combined food preparation and serving workers receive a part of their earnings as tips, fast-food workers usually do not.

Median hourly earnings of counter attendants in cafeterias, food concessions, and coffee shops (including tips) were $7.32 in 2002. The middle 50 percent earned between $6.52 and $8.53 an hour. The lowest 10 percent earned less than $5.87, and the highest 10 percent earned more than $10.39 an hour.

Median hourly earnings of dishwashers were $7.15 in 2002. The middle 50 percent earned between $6.40 and $8.28. The lowest 10 percent earned less than $5.82, and the highest 10 percent earned more than $9.41 an hour.

Median hourly earnings of nonrestaurant food servers were $7.52 in 2002. The middle 50 percent earned between $6.51 and $9.36. The lowest 10 percent earned less than $5.87, and the highest 10 percent earned more than $11.72 an hour.

Many beginning or inexperienced workers start earning the Federal minimum wage of $5.15 an hour. However, a few States set minimum wages higher than the Federal minimum. Also, various minimum wage exceptions apply under specific circumstances to disabled workers, full-time students, youth under age 20 in their first 90 days of employment, tipped employees, and student-learners. Tipped employees are those who customarily and regularly receive more than $30 a month in tips.

The employer may consider tips as part of wages, but the employer must pay at least $2.13 an hour in direct wages. Employers also are permitted to deduct from wages the cost, or fair value, of any meals or lodging provided. Many employers, however, provide free meals and furnish uniforms. Food and beverage service workers who work full time often receive typical benefits, while part-time workers usually do not.

In some large restaurants and hotels, food and beverage serving and related workers belong to unions—principally the Hotel Employees and Restaurant Employees International Union and the Service Employees International Union.

ROLE OF MANAGERS

Food service managers are responsible for the daily operations of restaurants and other establishments that prepare and serve meals and beverages to customers. Besides coordinating activities among various departments, such as kitchen, dining room, and banquet operations, food service managers ensure that customers are satisfied with their dining experience. In addition, they oversee the inventory and ordering of food, equipment, and supplies and arrange for the routine maintenance and upkeep of the restaurant, its equipment, and facilities. Managers generally are responsible for all of the administrative and human-resource functions of running the business, including recruiting new employees and monitoring employee performance and training.

In most full-service restaurants and institutional food service facilities, the management team consists of a *general manager*, one or more *assistant managers*, and *an executive chef*. The executive chef is responsible for all food preparation activities, including running kitchen operations, planning menus, and maintaining quality standards for food service. In limited-service eating places, such as sandwich shops, coffee bars, or fast-food establishments, managers, not executive chefs, are responsible for supervising routine food preparation operations.

Assistant managers in full-service facilities generally oversee service in the dining rooms and banquet areas. In larger restaurants and fast-food or other food service facilities that serve meals daily and maintain longer hours, individual assistant managers may supervise different shifts of workers. In smaller restaurants, formal titles may be less important, and one person may undertake the work of one or more food service positions. For example, the executive chef also may be the general manager or even sometimes an owner.

One of the most important tasks of food service managers is assisting executive chefs as they select successful menu items. This task varies by establishment depending on the seasonality of menu items, the frequency with which restaurants change their menus, and the introduction of daily or weekly specials. Many restaurants rarely change their menus while others make frequent alterations.

Managers or executive chefs select menu items, taking into account the likely number of customers and the past popularity of dishes. Other issues considered when planning a menu include whether there was any unserved food left over from prior meals that should not be wasted, the need for variety, and the seasonal availability of foods. Managers or executive chefs analyse the recipes of the dishes to determine food, labour, and overhead costs and to assign prices to various dishes. Menus must be developed far enough in advance that supplies can be ordered and received in time.

Managers or executive chefs estimate food needs, place orders with distributors, and schedule the delivery of fresh food and supplies. They plan for routine services or deliveries, such as linen services or the heavy cleaning of dining rooms or kitchen equipment, to occur during slow times or when the dining room is closed. Managers also arrange for equipment maintenance and repairs, and coordinate a variety of services such as waste removal and pest control.

Managers or executive chefs receive deliveries and check the contents against order records. They inspect the quality of fresh meats, poultry, fish, fruits, vegetables, and baked goods to ensure that expectations are met. They meet with representatives from restaurant supply companies and place orders to replenish stocks of tableware, linens, paper products, cleaning supplies, cooking utensils, and furniture and fixtures.

Managers must be good communicators. They need to speak well, often in several languages, with a diverse clientele and staff. They must motivate employees to work as a team, to ensure that food and service meet appropriate standards. Managers also must ensure that written supply orders are clear and unambiguous.

Managers interview, hire, train, and, when necessary, fire employees. Retaining good employees is a major challenge facing food service managers. Managers recruit employees at career fairs, contact schools that offer academic programmes in hospitality or culinary arts, and arrange for newspaper advertising to attract additional applicants. Managers oversee the training of new employees and explain the establishment's policies and practices. They schedule work hours, making sure that enough workers are present to cover each shift. If employees are unable to work, managers may have to call in alternates to cover for them or fill in themselves when needed. Some managers may help with cooking, clearing tables, or other tasks when the restaurant becomes extremely busy.

Food service managers ensure that diners are served properly and in a timely manner. They investigate and resolve customers' complaints about food quality or service. They monitor orders in the kitchen to determine where backups may occur, and they work with the chef to remedy any delays in service. Managers direct the cleaning of the dining areas and the washing of tableware, kitchen utensils, and equipment to comply with company and government sanitation standards.

Managers also monitor the actions of their employees and patrons on a continual basis to ensure the personal safety of everyone. They make sure that health and safety standards and local liquor regulations are obeyed. In addition to their regular duties, food service managers perform a variety of administrative assignments, such as keeping employee work records, preparing the payroll, and completing paperwork to comply with licensing laws and reporting requirements of tax, wage and hour, unemployment compensation, and Social Security laws. Some of this work may be delegated to an assistant manager or bookkeeper, or it may be contracted out, but most general managers retain responsibility for the accuracy of business records. Managers also maintain records of supply and equipment purchases and ensure that accounts with suppliers are paid.

Technology influences the jobs of food service managers in many ways, enhancing efficiency and productivity. Many restaurants use computers to track orders, inventory, and the seating of patrons. Point-of-service (POS) systems allow servers to key in a customer's order, either at the table, using a hand-held device, or from a computer terminal in the dining room, and send the order to the kitchen instantaneously so preparation can begin. The same system totals and prints checks, functions as a cash register, connects to credit card authorizers, and tracks sales.

To minimise food costs and spoilage, many managers use inventory-tracking software to compare the record of sales from the POS with a record of the current inventory. Some establishments enter an inventory of standard ingredients and suppliers into their POS system. When supplies of particular ingredients run low, they can be ordered directly from the supplier using preprogrammed information. Computers also allow restaurant and food service managers to keep track of employee schedules and paychecks more efficiently.

Food service managers use the Internet to track industry news, find recipes, conduct market research, purchase supplies or equipment, recruit employees, and train staff. Internet access also makes service to customers more efficient. Many restaurants maintain Web sites that include menus and online promotions, provide information about the restaurant's location, and offer patrons the option to make a reservation.

Managers tally the cash and charge receipts received and balance them against the record of sales. They are responsible for depositing the day's receipts at the bank or securing them in a safe place. Finally, managers are responsible for locking up the establishment, checking that ovens, grills, and lights are off, and switching on alarm systems.

Working Situations

Food service managers are among the first to arrive in the morning and the last to leave at night. Long hours—12 to 15 per day, 50 or more per week, and sometimes 7 days a week—are common. Managers of institutional food service facilities, such as school, factory, or office cafeterias, work more regular hours because the operating hours of these establishments usually conform to the operating hours of the business or facility they serve. However, hours for many managers are unpredictable.

Managers should be calm, flexible, and able to work through emergencies, such as a fire or flood, in order to ensure everyone's safety. Managers also should be able to fill in for absent workers on short notice. Managers often experience the pressures of simultaneously coordinating a wide range of activities. When problems occur, it is the manager's responsibility to resolve them with minimal disruption to customers. The job can be hectic, and dealing with irate customers or uncooperative employees can be stressful.

Managers also may experience the typical minor injuries of other restaurant workers, such as muscle aches, cuts, or burns. They might endure physical discomfort from moving tables or chairs to accommodate large parties, receiving and storing daily supplies from vendors, or making minor repairs to furniture or equipment.

Job Opportunities

Food service managers held about 386,000 jobs in 2002. Most managers were salaried, but about one-third were self-employed in independent restaurants or other small food service establishments. Almost three-fourths of all salaried jobs for food service managers were in full-service restaurants or limited-service eating places, such as fast-food restaurants and cafeterias. Other salaried jobs were in drinking places (alcoholic beverages) and in special food services—an industry that includes food service contractors who supply food services at institutional, governmental, commercial, or industrial locations. A small number of salaried jobs were in traveler accommodation (hotels); educational services; amusement, gambling, and recreation industries; nursing care facilities; and hospitals. Jobs are located throughout the country, with large cities and tourist areas providing more opportunities for full-service dining positions.

Training

Most food service management companies and national or regional restaurant chains recruit management trainees from 2-and 4-year college hospitality management programmes. Restaurant chains prefer to hire people with degrees in restaurant and institutional food service management, but they often hire graduates with degrees in other fields who have demonstrated interest and aptitude. Some restaurant and food service manager positions—particularly self-service and fast-food—are filled by promoting experienced food and beverage preparation and service workers. Waiters, waitresses, chefs, and fast-food workers demonstrating potential for handling increased responsibility sometimes advance to assistant manager or management trainee jobs. Executive chefs need extensive experience working as chefs, and general managers need prior restaurant experience, usually as assistant managers.

A bachelor's degree in restaurant and food service management provides particularly strong preparation for a career in this occupation. A number of colleges and universities offer 4-year programmes in restaurant and hotel management or institutional food service management. For those not interested in pursuing a 4-year degree, community and junior colleges, technical institutes, and other institutions offer programmes in the field leading to an associate degree or other formal certification. Both 2- and 4-year programmes provide instruction in subjects such as nutrition, sanitation, and food planning and preparation, as well as accounting, business law and management, and computer science. Some programmes combine classroom and laboratory study with internships providing on-the-job experience. In addition, many educational institutions offer culinary programmes in food preparation. Such training can lead to a career as a cook or chef and provide a foundation for advancement to an executive chef position.

Most restaurant chains and food service management companies have rigorous training programmes for management positions. Through a combination of classroom and on-the-job training, trainees receive instruction and gain work experience in all aspects of the operation of a restaurant or institutional food service facility. Areas include food preparation, nutrition, sanitation, security, company policies and procedures, personnel management, recordkeeping, and preparation of reports. Training on use of the restaurant's computer system is increasingly important as well. Usually, after 6 months or a year, trainees receive their first permanent assignment as an assistant manager.

Most employers emphasise personal qualities when hiring managers. For example, self-discipline, initiative, and leadership ability are essential. Managers must be able to solve problems and concentrate on details. They need good communication skills to deal with customers and suppliers, as well as to motivate and direct their staff. A neat and clean appearance is important, because managers must convey self-confidence and show respect in dealing with the public. Food service management can be physically demanding, so good health and stamina also are important.

The certified Foodservice Management Professional (FMP) designation is a measure of professional achievement for food service managers. Although not a requirement for employment or advancement in the occupation, voluntary certification provides recognition of professional competence, particularly for managers who acquired their skills largely on the job. The National Restaurant Association Educational Foundation awards the FMP designation to managers who achieve a qualifying score on a written examination, complete a series of courses that cover a range of food service management topics, and meet standards of work experience in the field.

Willingness to relocate often is essential for advancement to positions with greater responsibility. Managers typically advance to larger establishments or regional management positions within restaurant chains. Some eventually open their own food service establishments.

Employment of food service managers is expected to grow about as fast as the average for all occupations through 2012. In addition to job openings arising out of employment growth, the need to replace managers who transfer to other occupations or stop working will create many job opportunities. Applicants with a bachelor's or an associate degree in restaurant and institutional food service management should have the best job opportunities.

Projected employment growth varies by industry. Most new jobs will arise in full-service restaurants and limited-service eating places as the number of these establishments increases along with the population. Manager jobs in special food services, an industry that includes food service contractors, will increase as hotels, schools, healthcare facilities, and other businesses contract out their food services to firms in this industry. Food service manager jobs still are expected to increase in hotels, schools, and health-care facilities, but growth will be slowed as contracting out becomes more common.

Job opportunities should be better for salaried managers than for self-employed managers. More new restaurants are affiliatcd with national chains than are independently owned and operated. As this trend continues, fewer owners will manage restaurants themselves, and more restaurant managers will be employed by larger companies to run individual establishments.

Wages

Median annual earnings of salaried food service managers were $35,790 in 2002. The middle 50 percent earned between $27,910 and $47,120. The lowest 10 percent earned less than $21,760, and the highest 10 percent earned more than $67,490. Median annual earnings in the industries employing the largest numbers of food service managers in 2002 were as follows:

Special food services	$40,720
Traveler accommodation	39,210
Full-service restaurants	37,280
Nursing care facilities	33,910
Limited-service eating places	33,590
Elementary and secondary schools	31,210

In addition to receiving typical benefits, most salaried food service managers are provided free meals and the opportunity for additional training, depending on their length of service.

12

Retail Liquor Industry

Liquor industry has a three tiered system for the distribution of its products. The first tier is the manufacturer, the second tier is the distributor or wholesaler, and the third tier is the retailer. The manufacturer sells or grants licenses based on different criteria. The manufacturer may or may not be located in the state. Each state controls what products may be brought into its borders. The distributor or wholesaler sells and distributes the products to the retailers.

The basic merchandise carried by the stores are wine, liquor, and beer. The stores usually carry some, if not all, of the following: cigarettes, soda, chips, drink mixes, cheeses, and spring water. Many upscale stores have extensive wine departments with a wine expert on hand. Some small liquor stores are more of a grocery store than a traditional package store.

In recent years, total liquor consumption has been steadily declining due to changes in social attitude toward alcohol consumption as well as tougher governmental regulation and enforcement. Because of recent tort cases the usual liquor store will have few assets. The assets will usually consist of equipment needed to operate the business and inventory. Real property is usually held by the shareholder directly or indirectly to protect the assets in a law suit. Many stores may not have liability insurance because the premiums are so high.

A Case Study of Massachuseits Liquor Industry

The Massachusetts liquor industry consists of almost 4,000 liquor stores that are, for the most part, small independently owned stores. The State places many restrictions on these owners. Individuals may only own three licenses at a time. These licenses cannot be owned by an individual who is not a resident of the State or by an out of State corporation. However, a corporation may have out of State shareholders. A few larger stores operate as franchises. The owner will usually have two store licenses and one license for a warehouse.

The warehouse provides liquor for its own stores and other stores paying or participating in the franchise operation. The State places many restrictions on these stores; such as, the hours and days they may be open, who they may sell their product to, who they can purchase this product from and how they may transport it. The State allows the stores to be open Monday through Saturday and selected holidays. Stores on the New Hampshire border can be open on Sundays. They cannot open before 8:00 a.m. and must close by 11:00 p.m. These stores cannot sell to other liquor stores, bars, and any other entity set up like a bar, that is, Elks club etc.

The State also restricts their ability to purchase liquor products from anyone other than a liquor distributor located in the State of Massachusetts. The State requires different types of licenses in order for a business to sell or distribute liquor products. For example, a Section 22 license is required in order to transport liquor, wine, and beer products.

A price book, *The Massachusetts Beverage Price Journal*, published monthly, lists the purchase price for all liquor products sold in the State. The wholesalers must sell the product to the liquor store at this price. Larger stores receive free goods or cash credits for large quantities purchased. These are acceptable practices if reported to the State. However, Massachusetts will not allow a store to sell alcoholic beverages below cost. The State has investigators who check on these transactions.

In the State of Massachusetts, most liquor stores have lottery sales. Your state lottery commission is a potential source of information to verify the reported lottery income and test the store's internal controls.

In Massachusetts, there is a 5 cent deposit on most beer and soft drink bottles. Depending on whether bottle/ can redemption is required in the state, another source of information would be the bottle redemption centers.

The industry has several associations. It has a national organization that has a large membership. In addition, many states have their own associations. In Massachusetts one of these is the Massachusetts Package Stores Association. This association's primary purpose is to work on State legislation that affects the liquor industry. Approximately 30 percent of the liquor store industry in the State are members of this association. The association also offers group benefits for its members; such as, health insurance plans, workers compensation packages, credit card programs, and discounts on paper goods (register tapes etc.). In addition, the association issues membership bulletins regularly to keep its members informed of current issues.

The alcoholic beverage regulatory agency, in your state, can be a good source of information. They should be able to provide you with the number of licenses held and what reporting requirements there are. There are also local guides that may be of assistance. In Massachusetts, for example, the Massachusetts Continuing Legal Education group publishes a book called Entertainment and Alcoholic Licensing.

Industry Practices

In the retail liquor store industry there are many common practices. These practices are explained below to assist the examiners in familiarizing themselves with the industry.

Accounting systems

The retail liquor stores keep books and records that are similar to most small retail stores. The smaller stores maintain their records using a one write system. The larger stores maintain a general ledger, a cash receipts/sales journal and a cash disbursements/purchases journal. The larger stores also maintain other schedules such as aged receivables and aged payables.

Beer sales

Beer is normally purchased in a package called a suitcase consisting of 24 cans. The liquor stores purchase plastic rings from the wholesalers and breakdown the suitcases into six packs by placing the cans in the rings. Also, boxes for the six packs can be bought from the wholesalers. By doing this the gross profit on the sale of the beer cans will increase since the sales price for individual cans, six packs and cases differ.

Bottle redemptions

In Massachusetts, there is a 5 cent bottle deposit on most bottles and cans, purchased and sold. The State requires the wholesalers to pay 2.25 cent plus the bottle deposit of

5 cent to the liquor stores redeeming the bottles. In addition, the State requires the wholesalers to provide pick up services for the empty bottles redeemed. Some wholesalers pick up the bottles themselves and some hire a recycling company to pick up the bottles. If the wholesaler uses a recycling company the liquor store receives the bottle redemption income from the recycling company.

Lottery sales

Many retail liquor stores sell lottery tickets to bring customers into their stores. There are three categories of lottery games in Massachusetts. These lottery games are:

1. Lotto games—Megabucks, Mass Millions, Mass Cash and The Numbers Game
2. Instant games—$1, $2 and $5 instant tickets
3. Keno

In Massachusetts, all sales agents receive a 5 percent commission on all lottery sales. In addition, they receive a 1 percent bonus on all prizes paid under $600. The agents also receive other bonuses on higher tier prizes over $600 and on yearly ticket renewals. Each State may have its own lottery system.

Other income items

The retail liquor stores sell primarily liquor products, however, they do sell other items. These consist of seasonal items, glassware, snack foods, cigarettes, etc. Cigarettes are displayed on racks based on brand. A commission may be paid to the store based on brand placement. The commission is small and is usually only given for top shelf space.

Fine wine departments

Many larger retail liquor stores have fine wine departments. These departments market toward the sophisticated wine customer. There is a wine director who is responsible for fine wine purchases. The director is also available for consultations with the customers to help them select the appropriate wine. The wine director often publishes a wine newsletter for store customers. These newsletters provide information on the best wines available and on promotions in the stores. The wine directors rely on magazine articles, wine tasteings, and other sources for the information they provide.

Advertising

Advertising is done at national and local levels. The manufacturers will advertise their product nationally on television and in magazines. The retail liquor stores advertise primarily in the local and statewide newspapers. Some will do radio advertising. Often, several stores will get together and place one advertisement for sale items. The newspaper will bill a store and the other stores will reimburse that store for their share of the expense. Most of the larger stores advertise sales every week.

Scanning registers

Scanning cash registers are a new item in the retail liquor stores in Massachusetts. Due to the cost involved, most stores did not find it cost effective to purchase this type of cash register. These registers offer a perpetual inventory system by reading a UPC label at point of sale. It provides increased controls on the store inventory and on the store sales. It also can be used to assist in the purchasing needs of the store.

Security

Many store owners find that their biggest security problems are with their employees. There are several ways the stores "keep an eye" on their employees. One of them is the use of surveillance cameras. Another type of security used is undercover shoppers who watch he cashier as they ring in sales. During the busy seasons, Christmas and New Years, stores use police details to protect against shoplifting. Since this is a cash business most stores have some type of security system in place.

Deliveries

In Massachusetts, some retail liquor stores deliver to customers. Liquor cannot be transported without a license. One license is required for each delivery vehicle. The delivery vehicle is often a van or a vehicle that the owner of the store drives.

Customers on account

Most of the retail liquor stores give credit to customers who frequent their stores. There are several ways to account for these sales. Some stores ring the sale into the cash register at the time of the purchase, some accumulate sales slips and ring them in once or twice a month, and some stores ring in the sale at the time of payment. The method of accounting for these sales should be determined during the initial interview. The store should record the sales on consecutively numbered sales invoices. In addition, if the sales are rung in the cash register at the time of payment there should be a year end adjusting entry bringing the receivables into income.

Beer coolers

It is important to note that normally the largest asset of a retail liquor store is the beer cooler. Large maintenance and repair expenses may be found to keep the cooler in good working order.

Income Examinations

Retail liquor stores are cash intensive businesses. Therefore, the examiner should consider performing an in-depth probe for income.

Sales Beer, Wine and Liquors

Generally, liquor stores in Massachusetts will sell beer, wine and liquor. However, some stores may sell only beer and wine. Usually, each product is marked up separately and the markup is based on the owner's expertise and knowledge of the items. Massachusetts State law does not allow a liquor store to sell an item below cost. Many liquor stores also sell cigarettes, snacks, and mixes.

Books and records

Daily cash receipts are recorded on a daily sales sheet. The z total on the cash register tape is generally the sales figure recorded. The z total is the total amount of sales for the day by item and is generally run at the end of the day. Also recorded on the daily sales sheet are cash paid out for bottles and other items, bottle deposits, and the net bank deposit.

The daily sales sheets are posted to a weekly or monthly summary. This summary is usually in a spreadsheet format and contains the totals from the daily sales sheets. The summaries are posted to a trial balance or a general ledger at year end and finally to the tax return. Items such as commission income and bottle redemption income, are separate items on the daily sales sheets.

Issues

Income issues may be caused by an inaccurate posting from the daily sheets to the summaries or from the summaries to the trial balance or tax return. Cash paid out may not be included in the computation of gross receipts if the taxpayer uses a bank deposit method to determine income.

Another issue the team encountered was employee embezzlement. Many store owners stated that this was one of their biggest problems. It is usually an employee that has been with the store for a length of time and has learned their system. The agent will need to determine whether the embezzlement was of cash or inventory. If it is inventory, no corporate adjustments will be necessary since the year end inventory should have taken this into account. If cash was taken, the agent will need to determine whether it was taken prior to or after being rung into the register. Employee embezzlement will affect the store's gross profit percentage. The embezzlement income is taxable to the employee.

Bottle Redemption Income

Massachusetts State law requires a 5 cent deposit for all bottles and cans sold by retail and wholesale establishments. The wholesaler will collect the deposit on sales to the retailer. The retailer will then collect the deposit from the customer. Customers who turn in empty cans and bottles to a retailer will receive either cash or a credit on a future purchase. The retailer will then return the bottles and cans to a wholesaler or to an independent redemption company. The retailer will receive a 7.25 cent purchase credit or cash payment for every bottle and can returned.

Books and records

Generally, the daily sales sheets reflect bottle redemption income. The daily sales shects will show both the deposits collected and the cash paid out for bottles and cans turned in. These sales sheets should reconcile to the bank deposits and the cash register tapes.

The bottles turned into the wholesaler should be accounted for as a credit on a subsequent purchase invoice. If bottles and cans are collected by a redemption company, the liquor store will receive a check for the redemption income.

Issues

The major issue involved in bottle redemption is income received from independent bottle redemption companies. Liquor stores that receive bottle redemption checks may not deposit the check into the business account or may cash the check out of the daily cash receipts. A secondary issue is the improper recording of cash paid out. If bank deposits are used to determine income, cash paid out must be added to total deposits to arrive at gross receipts.

Audit techniques

When examining the bottle redemption issue, the daily sales sheets should be reconciled to the cash register tapes and the tapes to the sales sheets. The deposit slips should be scanned for large checks deposited that might indicate the taxpayer is cashing redemption checks out of the cash register and not reporting their receipt. When conducting a bank deposit analysis all cash paid out should be added to deposits to arrive at gross receipts.

Lottery Income

The lottery in Massachusetts consists of three games: Lotto

Games, Instant Games, and Keno. The liquor store receives a 5 percent commission on all lottery sales. In addition, they receive a 1 percent bonus on all prizes paid under $600. The bonuses paid on higher tier prizes, over $600, may be different. Each sales agent should keep a separate bank account for lottery transactions. This account should receive deposits for daily sales. The lottery then withdraws from the account the amount due them, net of commissions and bonuses. Often, the sales agent deposits only the net amount due to the lottery into this account.

Books and records

In Massachusetts, the lotto games and keno have a weekly sales report called SR61. The SR61 report, generated by the sales agent's lottery machine, shows sales, commissions, bonuses, and claims for the week. The instant games have an "Agent Issuance and Settlement Form" and a weekly sales report called SR31. The lottery representative prepares the "Agent Issuance and Settlement Form" every 2 weeks. The Form reconciles the sales agent's inventory held on a consignment basis. The SR31 reconciles the games sales, commissions, and bonuses.

Issues

The major issue is the improper accounting of lottery commission and bonuses for fiscal year taxpayers.

Audit techniques

Third party contacts should be made with the lottery commission to verify bonuses and commissions earned. For calendar year taxpayers, the Form 1099 issued by the State should be reconciled to lottery income reported.

Cost of Goods Sold

Generally, cost of goods sold is the largest deduction on a retail liquor store's tax return. Therefore, consider an in-depth examination of this item.

Purchases

The most common items found under the category of purchases are as follows: beer, wine, liquor, cigarettes, nuts, chips, pretzels, soda, candy, etc. Beer, wine, and liquor purchases make up most of the expense. Most retail stores deal with four to five major suppliers and several smaller suppliers. A less common purchase item is wine futures. This is a contract to purchase wine to be delivered at a later date and at a predetermined price.

Books and records

The smaller stores usually maintain their books using a one-write system. The larger stores maintain accounts payable and purchase journals. Most stores maintain daily records on a cash basis and make adjusting entries for accruals. Invoices, canceled checks, and paid out slips should be available to tie to the book entries. Wine futures may be evident on the balance sheet and should be supported by written contracts.

Issues

The general rule is that a liquor stores cannot include in inventory the amount paid for wine futures until they receive the wine. The amount paid should be reflected as an asset on the balance sheet. Given the recent promulgation of regulations under IRC sections 446 and 1221 concerning the tax treatment of hedging transactions, agents finding this issue on a return should make a referral to the financial products group in their district.

The team used two types of confirmation letters to confirm purchases as reported on the returns examined. The confirmations resulted in no adjustments.

Audit techniques

IRM 4231 text 5(10)2.1 outlines audit techniques to use when examining the purchases account. The following is an excerpt from the Manual as it applies to retail liquor stores:

1. Review cut-off date. Determine if year end purchases are recorded in the proper accounting period.
2. Determine owner consumption.
3. Scan the purchases column in the cash disbursements book and look for items unusual in amount or for vendors not associated with the products sold by the taxpayer.
4. Review entries in the general ledger. Note and verify entries which originate from other than usual sources.
5. Test check recorded amounts with vendor's invoices and canceled checks. Look for personal expenses, capital expenses and fictitious or duplicate invoices.
6. If purchases are made from a related entity, review a representative number of transactions to determine if the following are present: (a) price in excess of fair market value, (b) excessive rebates and allowances and (c) goods and services not received.
7. Ascertain if merchandise, discounts, prizes, trips, etc., were received as a result of volume purchases.
8. Ensure bottle credits issued by wholesalers are accounted for correctly.

During the initial interview the taxpayer should be asked whether the store deals in wine futures. A pre-audit of the balance sheet should indicate the presence of this issue.

Request all contracts and determine if the taxpayer is accounting for the futures correctly.

Inventory

All retail liquor stores should have an inventory. The smaller ones usually take a physical count at year end. Some larger stores with scanner registers will have a perpetual computerized count. Inventory should be valued at the lower of cost or market. Some stores take inventory at retail and make year end adjustments to bring inventory value to cost. The method to bring the retail amount to cost varies and is based on the owner's expertise. Some stores may not have a system for taking inventory and the amount is based on an eyeball review of what was in the store. This method is not permissible.

Books and records

The IRM states that taxpayers should have inventory count sheets and computerized taxpayers should have computer run inventory sheets. In Massachusetts, there is a beverage price journal which lists the purchase price of liquor products purchased in the State. Each individual product usually has its own mark-up percentage. Therefore, a reconstruction of inventory based on a mark-up percentage may be difficult.

Issues

An issue found during examinations of small retail stores that filed Form 1120A was the omission of inventory from the cost of goods sold calculation. The cost of goods sold section on the return requires the taxpayer to only fill in the purchases amount and then refers the taxpayer to the instruction booklet to account for the beginning and ending inventory. As a result, the taxpayer deducts purchases as cost of goods sold without adjusting for inventory.

Another issue is the failure to keep any records to document ending inventory. Many owners state they know exactly what is in their store at any time just by looking around and fail to take a physical year end inventory. Also, some taxpayers taking inventory at retail use an arbitrary mark-up percentage and apply it across the board to all items in their inventory.

Audit techniques

IRM 4231 text 5(10)2.2 requires minimum checks when inventory is an examined item. The following are the checks that should be made:

a. Verify that the method of inventory valuation conforms to a prescribed method.

b. Compare inventory balances with prior and subsequent year returns and the taxpayer's books.

c. Check for unauthorized changes from cost to cost or market.

d. Check for gross profit percentage variations.

e. Check notes to financial statements of independent auditors.

f. Ensure year end purchases are included in ending inventory.

g. Determine if there have been any inventory write-downs to below cost.

If purchases and cost of goods sold are the same, then the taxpayer did not consider beginning and ending inventory balances when computing cost of goods sold. Most taxpayers in this situation have inventory balances on the balance sheet which may be used to make the adjustment. This is a change in accounting method.

A Uniform Capitalisation Rules

IRC section 263A requires any retail establishment with an average of gross receipts over $10 million over the past 3 years to capitalize certain indirect expenses into ending inventory. Most liquor stores do not meet the gross receipts test.

Books and records

There should be an adjusting entry for the amount determined under IRC section 263A. There also should be work papers with the computation to support the adjustment. The accounts payable or cash disbursements book along with the general ledger will document the dollar amounts on the computation work paper.

Issues

Some liquor stores are required to calculate the IRC section 263A adjustment in determining ending inventory. Those that are may not be calculating it at all or may be applying it incorrectly.

Audit techniques

Review the current and prior 2 years to obtain an average gross receipts to determine if IRC section 263A applies. If it does apply, request the adjusting entries and work papers used to calculate the adjustment. Ensure that the taxpayer has accounted for all includible costs and has applied an appropriate absorption ratio to these costs.

EXPENSES

The team examined all expense items. The following is a brief description of each expense and a discussion of the applicable issues.

Compensation of officers

Most retail liquor stores are closely held corporations and generally the officers are also the majority shareholders. The officers/shareholders are generally involved either directly or indirectly in the operations of the liquor store. Therefore, they are entitled to reasonable compensation.

Salaries and Wages

Most retail liquor stores are open at least 6 days a week. Due to the long hours of operation most retail liquor stores have full and part time employees. Therefore, the liquor store would be entitled to deduct reasonable compensation. The team did not identify any significant issues in this expense.

Repairs

Generally, retail liquor stores own or rent such assets as cash registers, refrigeration units, buildings, etc. that are used in the operation of the business. The taxpayer is allowed to deduct the cost of incidental repairs that neither materially add to the value of the property nor appreciably prolong its life, but keep it in an ordinarily efficient operating condition. Therefore, most repairs of these assets are ordinary and necessary expenses.

With most business tax returns there exists the potential for the taxpayer to expense an item that should be capitalized and depreciated. Generally, repairs in the nature of replacements should be capitalized and depreciated to the extent that they slow deterioration and appreciably prolong the life of the property. Review the invoices for large repair expenses to determine if properly handled.

Bad Debts

Retail liquor stores are cash intensive businesses. Generally, there are few sales on account. Therefore, the retail liquor store does not normally have bad debts. Any significant bad debt expense deduction warrants further investigation. The team did not identify any significant issues in this expense.

Rents

Some retail liquor stores lease or rent the building from which they operate out. The taxpayer is allowed to deduct reasonable rent expense. Typically, the shareholder owns the land and building used by the corporation. Therefore, rent is paid by the corporation to the shareholder. Since this is a related party transaction the corporation paying rent in excess of fair rental value is a potential issue.

The corporation benefits by paying out excess funds as deductible rents as opposed to a nondeductible dividend distribution. The shareholder also benefits on his or her personal tax return in that the income can be reduced by rental expenses. Rents determined to be paid in excess of fair rental value are disallowed on the corporate tax return and generally constitute constructive dividends on the shareholder's tax return (provided the corporation has adequate earnings and profits).

Passive income

The shareholder may generate passive income (gross rents less allowable expenses) from renting to the shareholder's controlled corporation. This passive income is then used to offset otherwise nondeductible passive losses.

Taxes

The following taxes may be paid by a retail liquor store:

payroll taxes, corporate state taxes, state sales taxes, state excise taxes, local property taxes, and Federal income taxes.

Interest

Assets purchased by a retail liquor store (inventory, refrigeration units, liquor license, etc.) generally require a substantial amount of money. It is usually necessary for the taxpayer to borrow at least a portion of the money and pay interest on the borrowed money. The reasonable interest paid on the business related loans is an allowable deduction.

Any money borrowed from a related party (shareholder, shareholder's relative, related corporation, etc.) should be scrutinized. There is the potential that the taxpayer could pay or receive interest in excess of a reasonable interest rate and avoid taxes by manipulating income and expenses.

Advertising

Many products a retail liquor store carries are nationally advertised by the manufacturers, such as Budweiser, Jack Daniels, etc. However it is still common for retail liquor stores to advertise locally. The retail liquor store may produce flyers or advertise with the local media such as newspapers, radio, and television. Advertising expenses should be reasonable in amount, have a reasonable relationship to the business, and be documented to be deductible.

Depreciation

Generally, retail liquor stores own various assets and are allowed to depreciate these assets. Typical assets that may be owned and used in the retail liquor business are:

refrigeration units, counters, shelves, cash registers, and buildings.

In many cases the retail liquor store leases the building. The lessee is responsible for leasehold improvements in many lease agreements. A potential issue exists if the retail liquor store is depreciating the leasehold improvements over the life of the lease as opposed to the life of the asset. Generally, leasehold improvements are considered improvements to real property. Therefore, use the asset life of commercial real property to calculate the depreciation expense.

Under the Modified Accelerated Cost Recovery System (MACRS) the cost of leasehold improvements made to real property are required to be depreciated without regard to the lease term (IRC section 168(i)(8)). For example, leasehold improvements made to commercial real property must be depreciated over 31.5 years.

Pensions and Profit Sharing Plans

Some retail liquor stores have a pension or profit-sharing plan set up for their employees. To examine for compliance with various pension and employee benefit rules, refer the case to an Employee Plans agent in your district. The following are some of the potential issues that should be referred to an Employee Plans agent.

Prohibited transactions

With a closely held corporation there exists the potential for "prohibited transactions" between the corporation and the pension plan. If a disqualified person borrows monies from the pension plan, this would be a prohibited transaction. The disqualified person is liable for an excise tax equal to 5 percent of the prohibited transaction amount. In addition, a 100 percent penalty will be assessed if the prohibited transaction is not corrected within the tax period.

Employee Benefit Plans

Generally, the only employee benefit program offered by retail liquor stores is health insurance for full-time employees and their families.

Automobile Expense

Some retail liquor stores deduct expenses relating to automobiles used in their business. Generally, the operation of a retail liquor store does not require substantial use of an automobile. Making deposits and picking up supplies are usually the only business related uses of an automobile. In Massachusetts, a taxpayer cannot pick up or deliver alcohol unless the taxpayer has a license that allows for the transportation of alcohol. Any automobile expenses that are determined to be personal expenses of the shareholder should be disallowed from the corporate tax return. A constructive dividend adjustment is also warranted using the annual lease value table. All other expenses incurred, in relation to the automobile, should be adjusted.

Insurance Expense

Most retail liquor stores have insurance coverage for liability, workmen's compensation, life, and auto insurance, etc. Scrutinize any insurance expenses that may be personal expenses of the shareholder such as life insurance and auto insurance. Any insurance expense that is disallowed as a personal expense of the shareholder should be charged to the shareholder as a constructive dividend if the corporation has adequate earnings and profits. There is no dividend distribution for the personal portion of auto insurance expense if the lease value method is used. The team made several adjustments to this expense.

Management Fees

Many retail liquor stores expensed management fees under other deductions. These fees are normally charged by a related corporation for services such as payroll and management. These services are often performed by the shareholder(s) of these stores.

Payments to a Related Party

In one case a taxpayer, who owned two retail liquor stores, set up a management company. The management company charged both retail liquor stores fees for consulting services. The management company then paid the shareholder and other employees as subcontractors. The management company did not withhold any payroll taxes. Payroll taxes were properly assessed against the management company.

Balance Sheet Examinations

Generally, examinations are conducted on income and expense accounts. In doing so, potential issues on the balance sheet may be overlooked. The following is a brief description and composition of the accounts encountered in the examination of the retail liquor stores. In addition, specific issues identified during the examinations are addressed. References are made to other areas of the audit techniques guide to supplement the information provided.

Assets

Cash

The cash account consists of the reconciled year end bank

account and petty cash balances. Generally, the retail liquor store will have two to three bank accounts: general checking, payroll, and lottery accounts. Although the State of Massachusetts requires the store to maintain a separate bank account for lottery transactions, some stores use one bank account for all income. Some liquor stores include the cash maintained in the cash register in this account, which usually stays the same throughout the year.

Withdrawals of corporate funds

While spinning the canceled checks of a closely-held liquor store, it was noted that there were no checks to the shareholder even though the shareholder received a salary and rental income. When questioned, the shareholder stated that he took cash from the register as needed. There were no records maintained for amounts withdrawn. However, most of the cash was deposited in the shareholder's personal account for the payment of personal expenses. Through a bank deposit analysis and personal living statement, the amount withdrawn was determined. Further analysis revealed that the corporation was making payments for some of the shareholder's personal expenses. It was determined that the shareholder received distributions from the corporation for the amounts withdrawn in excess of his salary and rental income reported.

Retail Inventory Method Incorrect

During the examination of a retail liquor store, a markdown reserve account was found. The taxpayer stated that the inventory had been valued using the retail inventory method.The taxpayer did not have specific markdown records. In addition, the computations used by the taxpayer to arrive at the ending inventory value were incorrect.

13

Revenue Control in Bar and Beverage Operations

Planning for and controlling revenue is just as important as properly managing costs. The last phase of the operational cycle is the collection of revenue for products and services offered to guests of the property. The first step in designing a control system for any resource, including revenue, is to set a standard. Revenue standards can then be compared against actual revenue.

One method is based upon guest checks. The standard-the amount of revenue a property expects to collect from its operations-is represented by the totals from guest checks for a specific meal period or periods. A second method relies on unit sales information entered into electronic register equipment before menu items are produced. The sum of this sales information defines revenue expectations.

Guest Check System

In some bar and beverage operations, a guest check system is at the heart of revenue control. The standard (expected) amount of revenue is represented by the total of all amounts recorded on individual guest checks for a meal period (or periods) after all checks have been accounted for. The reliability of this standard depends upon servers following strict procedures when processing individual guest checks. These procedures will depend on the degree of automation within the operation.

Manual Guest Check System

A fundamental revenue control procedure requires that servers neatly write all alcohol and beverage orders on guest checks. Servers generally use pens, not pencils, and mistakes must be crossed out rather than erased. In many operations, the server must have a supervisor initial a guest check that has items crossed out or voided. Before initialing, the supervisor makes sure that the deleted items were no prepared by kitchen or bar staff.

Before alcohol or beverage items are produced, servers must provide appropriate production staff with requisition slips. The server lists items on a requisitim slip and also records his or her name (or identification number) and the serial number of the corresponding guest check. Operations with manual guest check systerns typically use a duplicate guest check system for orders. With this system, each guest check has at least two parts.

The server turns in the duplicate, copy to the kitchen and keeps the original copy for presentation to the guest. When the guest is ready to pay, the guest check is tallied. A calculator with a printer that produces a tape should be used. The tape can be stapled to the check for the guest' review of charges. Requisition slips and duplicate checks are useful for routine guest check audio functions.

At the end of a meal period the manager (or designated staff) match requisition slips (or duplicate copies of guest checks) turned in to the kitchen with the corresponding guest checks for which revenue has been collected. This procedure identifies differences between what was produced and what was served. Routine audits of guest checks may also reveal mistakes made by servers in pricing items on guest checks or in calculating totals. These mistakes should be brought the attention of the responsible, staff members.

By conducting routine audits guest checks, management indicates to employees its concern about effective controlling the property's revenue collection system. Several other procedures apply to revenue control with a manual guest check system. Guest checks should be unique to the property. If guest checks are purchased from a local restaurant supply company, anyone-including dishonest employees-can buy them.

In this situation, guest checks can be used in the proper with no record of who has them or from whom revenue is due. Therefore, it is be to order specially printed, hard-to-duplicate guest checks. Unused checks should, be securely stored. They should not be left lying around in the manager's office at the host stand.

Guest checks should be sequentially numbered and a record kept of while checks are given to which employee. Beginning and ending numbers for all checks issued to servers should be listed on a guest check number log. Serve accepting the checks should verify receiving all checks for which they will be he accountable by signing the log.

All checks issued to each server must be accounted for at the end of a shifts. Checks will be either used and turned in with revenue, unused and turned in part of the server-closing procedures, or kept in use and transferred to another server. All transfers of guest checks should be approved by a supervisor.

Requisition slips or duplicate guest checks are helpful when a check is unaccounted for requisition slips (or the duplicate copy) corresponding to a missing guest checks have been turned in to the kitchen, management knows that the missing guest check has been used, that items listed on it have been served, and that revenue due from the server. According to property policy and in accordance with applicable wage and hour or other laws, penalties may be applied when checks are unaccounted for at the end of a server's shift.

Automated Guest Check System

Some automated systems use preprinted, serially numbered guest checks similar to those used by operations with manual guest check systems. Before entering an order, the server must "open" the guest check within the system. This is usually accomplished by inputting the server's identification number and the guest check's serial number.

Once the system has recognised the server and "opened" the guest check, orders are entered and relayed to remote printers located at appropriate production areas. Pre-check terminals are also equipped with guest check printers. As orders are relayed to production areas, the same items (with their selling prices) are printed on the server's guest check. Once a guest check has been opened, it becomes part of the system's open check file. For each opened guest check, this file may contain the following data:

— Terminal number where the guest check was opened

— Guest check serial number

— Server identification number

— Time guest check was opened

— Menu items ordered

— Prices of menu items ordered

— Applicable tax

— Total amount due

A server adds orders to the guest check at the pre check terminal by first inputting the guest check's serial number and then entering the additional items. There are many variations of this automated pre-checking system. Some systems use guest checks with bar codes corresponding to the preprinted serial numbers.

This eliminates the need for servers to input the guest check's serial number when opening a guest check or when adding items to guest checks already in use. When the guest check is placed in the guest check printer, the system reads the bar code and immediately accesses the appropriate file.

Modern systems eliminate the traditional guest check altogether. These systems maintain only an electronic file for each open guest check. A thin, narrow, recipe like guest check can be printed at any time during service, but is usually not printed until after the meal, when the server presents it to the guest for settlement. Since no paper forms are used, the table number often becomes the tracking identifier for the order. With some systems, seat numbers are used for tracking multiple checks per table.

Electronic cash registers and point-of-sale technology simplify guest check control functions and eliminate the need for most of the time-consuming manual audit procedures. Automated pre-checking functions eliminate mistakes made by servers in pricing items on guest checks or in calculating totals. When items must be voided after they have been entered into the system, a supervisor (with a special identification number) accesses the system and deletes the appropriate items.

Generally, automated systems produce a report that lists all guest transactions with voided or returned items, the servers responsible for each guest transaction, and the supervisors who accessed the system and voided the items.

It is important for automated systems to distinguish voided from returned items because returned items should be included in inventory usage reports, while voided items should not. If an item is voided after it has already been prepared, the item would be classified as "returned."

At any point in time, managers and/ or supervisors can access the system and monitor the status of any open transaction. This check-tracking capability can be used to help identify potential walkouts, reduce server fraud, and significantly tighten guest check and revenue control.

The status of a guest transaction changes from open to closed when payment is received from the guest and it is recorded in the system. Most automated systems produce an outstanding transaction report that lists all open transactions (by server). The sequence number, server identification number, time at which the transaction began, number of guests, table number, and guest check total. This data makes it much easier for managers to determine responsibility for open transactions.

Revenue Collection

The next step in revenue control is to develop and implement: revenue collection procedures to help ensure that actual revenue collected corresponds with defined revenue standards. Procedures in relation to two types of revenue collection systems: the server banking system and the cashier banking system. In addition, revenue reports produced by computerised point-of-sale systems are examined.

Server Banking System

With the server banking system, servers (and bartenders) use their own banks of money to collect payments from guests and retain the collected revenue until they check out at the end of their shifts. In some operations, locking cash boxes are provided for each server to store collected revenue, credit card vouchers, and other sales materials.

At the end of a shift, the amount of revenue duc the operation when a manual system is used is determined by tallying the totals from all guest checks assigned to each server. The tally is made by the manager (or cashier) in conjunction with the server. Totals from guest checks settled by credit card vouchers, personal checks, and house account charges are subtracted from the tally to arrive at the amount of cash to be collected from the server.

The remaining cash represents the server's opening change bank and any cash tips earned. After the actual revenue collected by the manager (or cashier) balances with the tally of totals from all guest checks assigned to the server, charged tips (as recorded on credit card or house account vouchers) are paid out to the server.

In nonautomated properties, these closing procedures can be very time- consuming. Electronic cash registers and point-of-sale technology speed up the process by producing a report at the end of a shift that automatically tallies the total revenue due from each server. The report generally identifies transactions opened by the server and itemises each of them in terms of:

— Table number
— Number of covers
— Elapsed time from opening to closing of the transaction
— Totals for alcohol and beverage revenue
— Tax
— Tips due
— Settlement method

Cashier Banking System

With the cashier banking system, guests pay the cashier, the bartender, or the alcohol or beverage server (who then pays the cashier or the bartender who has cashiering duties). Upon receiving a guest check for settlement, the cashier keys each item listed on the check into the register. The register tallies each item and imprints the total on the check for verification with the server's handwritten total.

With most electronic point-of-sale systems, the cashier does not have to key each item from every guest check into the register. The cashier's terminal simply accesses the transaction number opened by the server, and the cashier closes it by collecting and recording the revenue. At the end of the shift, the cashier's cash drawer and supporting documents are accounted for. The following sections focus on revenue collection procedures used by bar and beverage service operations with traditional cash register equipment.

At the end of the shift, cash register readings are taken and summarised. The cash, credit card vouchers, other types of payments, and any miscellaneous paid its are then reconciled with the cash register readings using a daily cashier's resort. An operation with several stations and shifts may find it more convenient to several daily cashier's reports, and summarise the data on a single report.

All daily cashier's reports are designed with common characteristics. These reports generally contain a heading showing the date and day of the week, and may contain information about the weather, number of guests, or other data helpful in analysing and managing the operation. They usually consist of separate sections for register readings, accounting of cash register funds and transactions, and supporting documents.

For internal control reasons, register readings are taken by the manager or a designated individual other than the cashier. The differences between beginning and ending readings less any "voids" (voided register entries approved by supervisors) represent alcohol/beverage revenue and sales taxes collected. The "To Be Accounted For" section represents net register readings, tips entered by guests on credit cards or charge accounts, collections from guests which are to be applied to prior balances of open accounts, and the initial change fund in the register. This section typically includes the following items:

— Alcohol/beverage revenue

— Sales tax

— Tips charged

— Guest collections

— Change fund (start)

The total of cash drawer funds and amounts represented on supporting documents should reconcile with this control total, except for minor cash shortages or overages. Minor shortages or overages are generally due to errors in processing the numerous cash transaction that an operation handles daily. Obviously, any large variances should be investigated for irregularities.

The "Accounted For" section represents the cash drawer funds, bankcard drafts, documents supporting items paid out 0 the cash drawer, and the return of the initial change fund (cash bank). This section typically includes the following items:

— Cash

— Purchases paid out

— Tips paid out

— Guest charges

— Change' fund/ cash bank (return)

— Cash shortages or overages

These total receipts and amounts paid out are reconciled with the control to and any minor cash shortages or overages are computed. The final "Total Accounted For" must reconcile with the total of the items. "To Be Accounted For" (the control total). Processing the "To Be Accounted For" Section. The "To Be Accounted For" section is processed as follows:

— Amounts for alcohol/beverage revenue and sales tax are the result of totals of register readings, less any void rings.

— Tips charged are tips that guests entered on credit card drafts or open account transactions.

— Guest collections are payments received from guests to be applied toward their prior charges on open accounts. These collections are explained in a listing on a separate section of the report.

— Change fund (start) represents the cashier's initial funds (cash bank) provided at the start of the day. This fund is a predetermined, fixed amount (also termed "imprest amount") established by management.

The total of the "To Be Accounted For" section serves as the control total. This control total will later be compared to the cash count and register documents to determine any cash shortages or overages. Processing the "Accounted For" Section. The "Accounted For" section is processed as follows:

— The change fund (cash bank) is restored to its original amount. The balance of the cash, personal checks, traveller's checks, and bank credit card drafts form the cash deposit.

— Purchases paid out represent incidentals that were paid from the cash drawer during the shift. The cashier supports these amounts paid out by including documented vouchers in the cash drawer. Paying for incidentals in this way eliminates the writing of checks for small items and averts the need for a separate cash fund.

— Tips paid out represent payments to employees for the tips that were entered on credit card drafts or open accounts. The policy of many operations is to pay the server immediately upon receipt of the credit card draft or open account charge. In this case, the net result of tips charged and tips paid out will be zero.

— Guest charges represent charges made by guests on their house accounts, and include the total of the guest checks. These charges are explained in a listing on a separate section of the report.

— The total of the above items, referred to as "Total Receipts and Paid Outs," is compared with the control total (the total of the "To Be Accounted For" section). Any difference between these two totals is due to a cash shortage or overage.

— The resulting "Accounted For" total must agree with the To Be Accounted For total (the control total).

Revenue Reports

Managers of automated alcohol and beverage operations benefit from the speed and accuracy by which revenue reports are produced. Revenue reports enable managers to measure the sales performance of individual menu items by product category within certain time intervals. These reports enable managers to track individual item sales, analyse product acceptance, and monitor advertising and sales promotional efforts.

The time intervals are commonly referred to as day parts. Day parts may vary in relation to the type of alcohol/beverage service operation. Fast-food restaurants may desire revenue analysis reports segmented by 15-minute intervals; table service restaurants, by the hour; and institutional alcohol/beverage service operations, by meal period. The information reported is used for forecasting revenue and determining labour requirements.

A revenue summary report generally contains detailed revenue and tax information by such categories as food items, beer, wine, and liquor. Generally, totals for each category are printed for each meal period, and totals for each meal period are shown in different sections of the report.

Productivity reports typically detail revenue activity for all assigned server revenue records. A daily productivity report may be generated for each server and cashier in terms of guest count, total revenue, and average revenue. In addition, a weekly productivity report may be generated, showing average revenue amount per guest for each server.

Standard Revenue

Just as in the control of alcohol/beverage revenue, the expected revenue from beverage sales is based on the total number of items actually sold. However, procedures for controlling beverage revenue are different from procedures for controlling alcohol/beverage revenue, and they are sometimes more complex to develop.

One reason for this is the difficulty of basing the control of beverage revenue on a guest check system. In properties with a nonautomated guest check system, procedures to control revenue include the following:

— The bartender is assigned guest checks at the start of a shift and must adhere to all requirements regarding their use. For example, when a guest at the bar or lounge table orders a drink, the bartender writes the order on a guest check.

— The bartender places the check face down on the bar or table in front of the guest and writes additional drink orders as necessary on the same check. If the bar cash register has an accounts receivable function, the bartender can ring the check through the machine before serving the drink.

— When the guest is ready to pay, the bartender rings the check into the register and deposits the funds.

— The bartender puts used guest checks in a locked check box until the end of the shift when they are accounted for.

— Totals from the guest checks are matched with register readings. Totals from all guest checks determine the standard expected revenue, which is compared to the actual revenue collected.

An obvious disadvantage of this method is the time required for the bartender to record guest check information. From a practical perspective, during busy rush periods, the procedure slows service. This is an excellent example of control procedures clashing with marketing and guest concerns.

The issue must be resolved by management based on the unique costs and benefits of each procedure in each specific operation. Another challenge in controlling beverage revenue is the impracticality of separating preparation, service, and collection activities. Bartenders frequently take an order, prepare and serve the drink, collect revenue, register the sale, and make change for guests.

The possibilities for theft of revenue are numerous since there are fewer opportunities for managers to ensure that all required revenue control procedures are being followed. One possibility is to define the standard revenue level for beverage sales in term's of a percentage of total revenue that managers have come to expect on the basis of past revenue records.

Managers of nonautomated beverage operations can use a number of methods to control beverage revenue. Many of these methods match the number of ounces of liquor used with the amount of revenue generated. Some of these methods can be very time-consuming. The following sections examine the bottle revenue value method, which is practical and yields reasonably accurate information. In addition, automated beverage control systems are discussed in relation to beverage revenue control and the types of reports that can be produced for beverage managers.

Bottle Revenue Value System

The bottle revenue value system involves estimating the amount of revenue expected from a bottle of liquor. The beverage income standard is determined from the number of empty liquor bottles. This standard is then compared with the amount of actual revenue generated. Differences represent the variance between standard and actual revenue.

For example, suppose that, at the end of a shift, three bottles of bar Scotch are issued in exchange for three empty bottles. If each empty bottle had a revenue value of $40, then $120 in revenue should have been generated from the sale of Scotch during the shift. This system does not account for changes in opened-bottle inventory, but instead assumes that the value of liquor in opened bottles evens out over time.

This method is easy to use, but its usefulness depends on how accurately bottle revenue values are determined. The procedure for calculating bottle revenue values involves examining the historical sales mix to establish a weighted average revenue value per bottle. This procedure assumes that the historical sales mix is an accurate predictor of current usage rates. The following sections examine a step-by-step procedure for implementing a bottle revenue value system.

Classify All Liquor by Type: Two common classifications are house and callliqliars. House liquor is served when no specific brand is ordered. Call liquor is that which is ordered by brand. (When, even more specific standard revenue information fur beverages is desired, it is possible to classify a third type of liquor-premium.)

Classify All Drinks by Kind: Two common classifications are mixed drinks and cocktails. Mixed drinks are liquor drinks to which a non-alcoholic mixer such as soda, tonic, or water is added. A cocktail is a drink made with two or more liquors or a drink containing a large amount of a single liquor.

Examine the Beverage Sales Mix: The beverage manager should establish a period of time to collect data about the beverage sales mix. Accuracy increases with the number of drinks reviewed. Review a proportionate number of 'drinks sold at all pricing periods. For example, if approximately 60 percent of all beverage revenue is generated from drinks sold at regular prices, then 60 percent of all drinks observed should be counted during regular price periods. Low- and high-price service times are other pricing periods that should be observed.

Count the Number of Each Type and Kind of Liquor Served: A count is kept of the number of each type (house or call) and kind (mixed drink or cocktail) of liquor served. Guest checks, register tapes, or physical counts can be used to tally the number of drinks served.

Determine the Revenue Value per Ounce: A revenue value per ounce calculation form can be used to determine the revenue value per ounce of house and call liquors. A count from sever allow pricing periods showed that 48 mixed drinks using house liquor were served.

The potential revenue values for each bottle of house liquor and each bottle of call liquor become the basis for defining standard beverage revenue levels when the number of empty bottles is counted at the end of each shift. All liter bottles of house liquor, whatever type, have the same revenue value. The same is true for all liter bottles of call liquor.

Most operations do not charge a different amount for each house liquor. The selling price of a mixed drink made with house liquor is generally the same regardless of whether it is made of Scotch, gin, or bourbon. The relationship between the cost of liquor and its selling price is less direct than the relationship between the cost of menu item and its selling price.

Furthermore, it would be impractical to manually keep track of all types of liquor and their different revenue values. In the procedure outlined above, information has to be assembled only for two types of liquor-house and call. To establish a bottle revenue value for each individual type of liquor would mean assessing sales information for the 70 to 100 different types and brands that might be carried by the beverage operation.

After the revenue value per bottle for house and call liquors is established, standard beverage revenue for liquor can be assessed. As full bottles are issued to replace empty bottles, the revenue value of each bottle is noted. A beverage issue and revenue value sheet is simply a modified version of the basic beverage requisition form. Using this form makes it easier to tally bottle revenue value information. The sum of revenue values for all bottles issued, is the standard revenue generated during the shift.

Automated Beverage Systems

Automated beverage systems significantly reduce many of the time-consuming management tasks for controlling beverage operations. While automated beverage systems vary, most systems can:

— Dispense drinks according to the operation's standard recipes

— Count the number of drinks poured

— Assess the standard (expected) revenue for beverage sales

— Provide timely management reports

Automated beverage systems can be programmed to dispense different portion sizes. They can also generate standard revenue information based on different pricing periods as defined by management. With most systems, the station at which drinks are prepared may be connected to a guest check printer that records every sale as drinks are dispensed.

Some systems require that a guest check be inserted into the printer before the drink will be dispensed. Most equipment can, and should, be connected to the bar cash register to automatically record all revenue generated through the automated equipment. With one type of automated beverage system, liquor is stored at the bar. Price coded pourers (special nozzles) are inserted into each bottle. These pourers cannot dispense liquor unless they are used with a special activator ring.

The bartender slips the neck of a liquor bottle (with the price-coded pourer already inserted) into the ring and prepares the drink with a conventional hand-pouring motion. A cord connects the activator ring to a master control panel that records the number of drinks poured at each price level. The master control panel may be connected to a point-of-sale system that records the sale.

Some master control panels are equipped with printers and can produce revenue reports for each station. Reports indicate the number of drinks poured at different price levels and the total standard (expected) revenue for each station.

With another type of automated beverage system, liquor is stored in racks in a locked storage room. The bartender prepares a drink by pushing the appropriate key on a keyboard. The liquor and necessary mixes travel to a dispensing device at the bar through separate plastic tubing. The system pours the drink when the bartender holds the glass (with ice) under the dispensing device.

The drink is then garnished and served to the guest. Extensive revenue and inventory reports can be produced with this type of system. Also, transactions can be tied to an automated transaction control system. For each shift and each station during a shift, separate reports can indicate:

— Revenues by major beverage category
— Revenues by time of day
— Revenues by server
— Settlement methods
— Outstanding guest checks
— Sales mix by beverage product

Unquestionably, automated beverage systems can greatly enhance management's control of beverage operations. At the least, the system can provide accurate information about the number of drinks and/or ounces sold. At best, such a system will not allow a drink to be served without its being entered as a sale within the system.

BIBLIOGRAPHY

Allen, H. Warner. *Natural Red Wines* with Report on the Red Wines of America by Frank Schoonmaker. Constable, London. Hardcover. 1951.

Carling, T. E. *Wine Lore - A Critical Analysis of Wine Dogma.* Practical Press Ltd. Surrey, UK. Hardcover Second Impression 1954. 55 pages.

Dahl, J. O. *Dictionary of 1001 menu terms, foods, wines, spirits, cocktails.* Stamford Conn: J. O. Dahl, 1935.

Elliot, Virginia. *Quiet drinking: a book of beer, wines & cocktails and what to serve with them.* New York: Harcourt, 1933.

Field, S. S., *The American Drink Book*. Farrar, Straus & Young. New York. First Printing, 1953.

Grohusko, J. A. *Jack's manual on the vintage and production, care and handling of wines, liquors, etc.: a* handbook of information for home, club, or hotel: recipes for fancy mixed drinks and when and how to *serve.* New York: McClunn & Co., 1910.

Hoggson, Noble Foster. *The Squire's Home-Made Wines as deserib'd and set-forth in the Journal of Thomas Hoggspm. Gent.*, 1765.

Hyams, Edward. *Dionysus: A Social History of the Wine Vine.* "A delightful and useful book for both the connoisseur and the novice." – Los Angeles Herald-Examiner. The MacMillan Co., NY. 128 Illus, 8 in colour. 1965.

Jackson, George H. *The Medicinal Value of French Brandy.* Printed by Therien Freres, Limitee, Montreal, Canada. 1928 Hardcover.

Langenbach, Alfred. *The Wines of Germany* , Harper & Co., London, 1951.

Pixley, Francis W. *Clubs and their management.* London New York etc: Sir I. Pitman & sons ltd., 1927.

Robb, Marshall J. *Scotch Whisky.* E. P. Dutton & Co., NY. 1951.

Schoonmaker, Frank and Tom Marvel. *The complete wine book.* New York: Simon and Schuster, 1934.

Street, Julian. *Wines: Their Selection Care and Service.* Alfred A Knopf Publisher, 194 pages + xx, Hardcover, Fold-out map, NY, 1933.

INDEX